Christmas 2002

For Christopher—

May you always have
Alex & bells on Christmas
Eve.

Uncle Carlos

Christmas
Traditions & Legends

Doris C. Baines

Illustrated By
Richard Ferguson

KD

KENDOR, Inc.

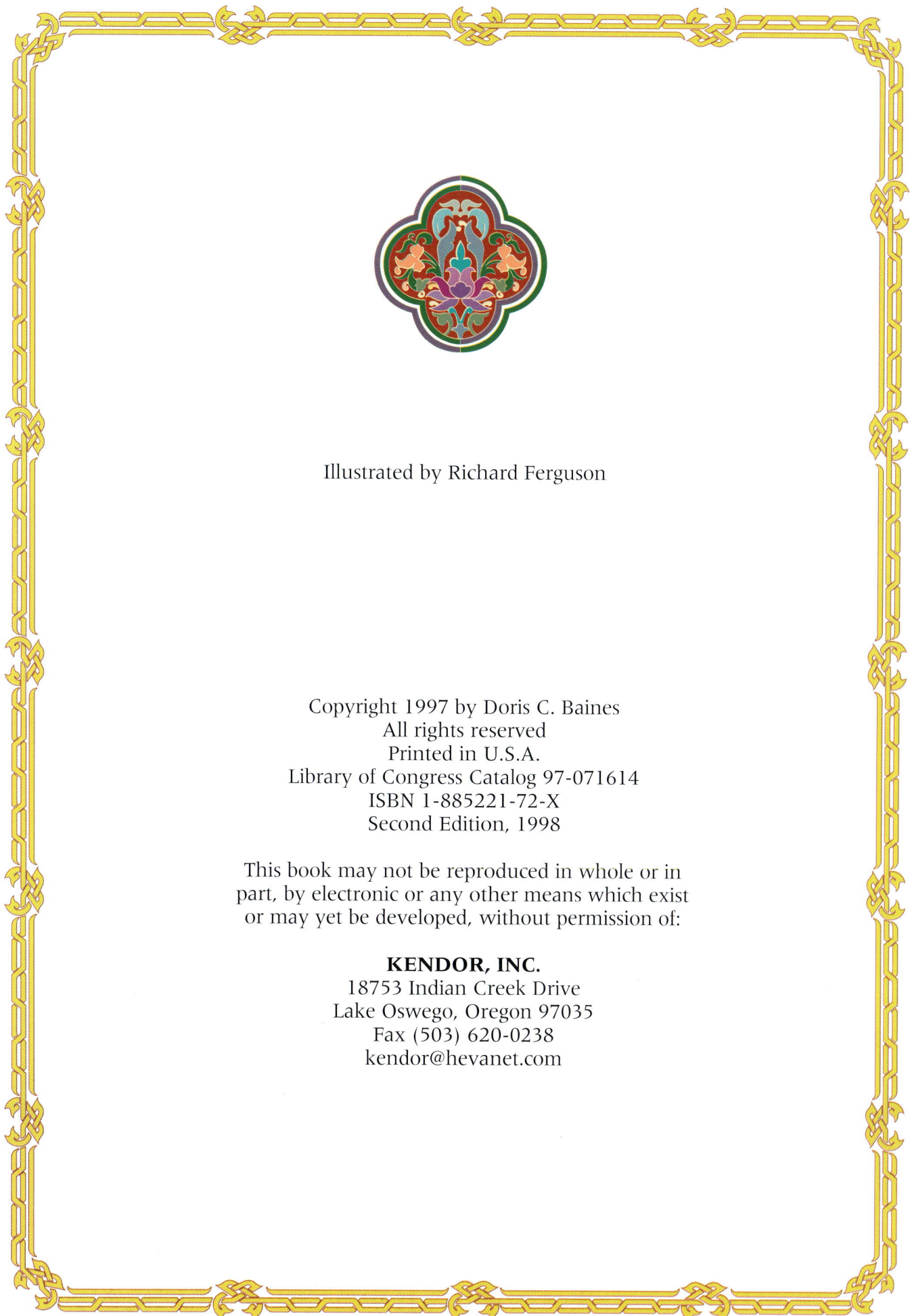

Illustrated by Richard Ferguson

Copyright 1997 by Doris C. Baines
All rights reserved
Printed in U.S.A.
Library of Congress Catalog 97-071614
ISBN 1-885221-72-X
Second Edition, 1998

This book may not be reproduced in whole or in part, by electronic or any other means which exist or may yet be developed, without permission of:

KENDOR, INC.
18753 Indian Creek Drive
Lake Oswego, Oregon 97035
Fax (503) 620-0238
kendor@hevanet.com

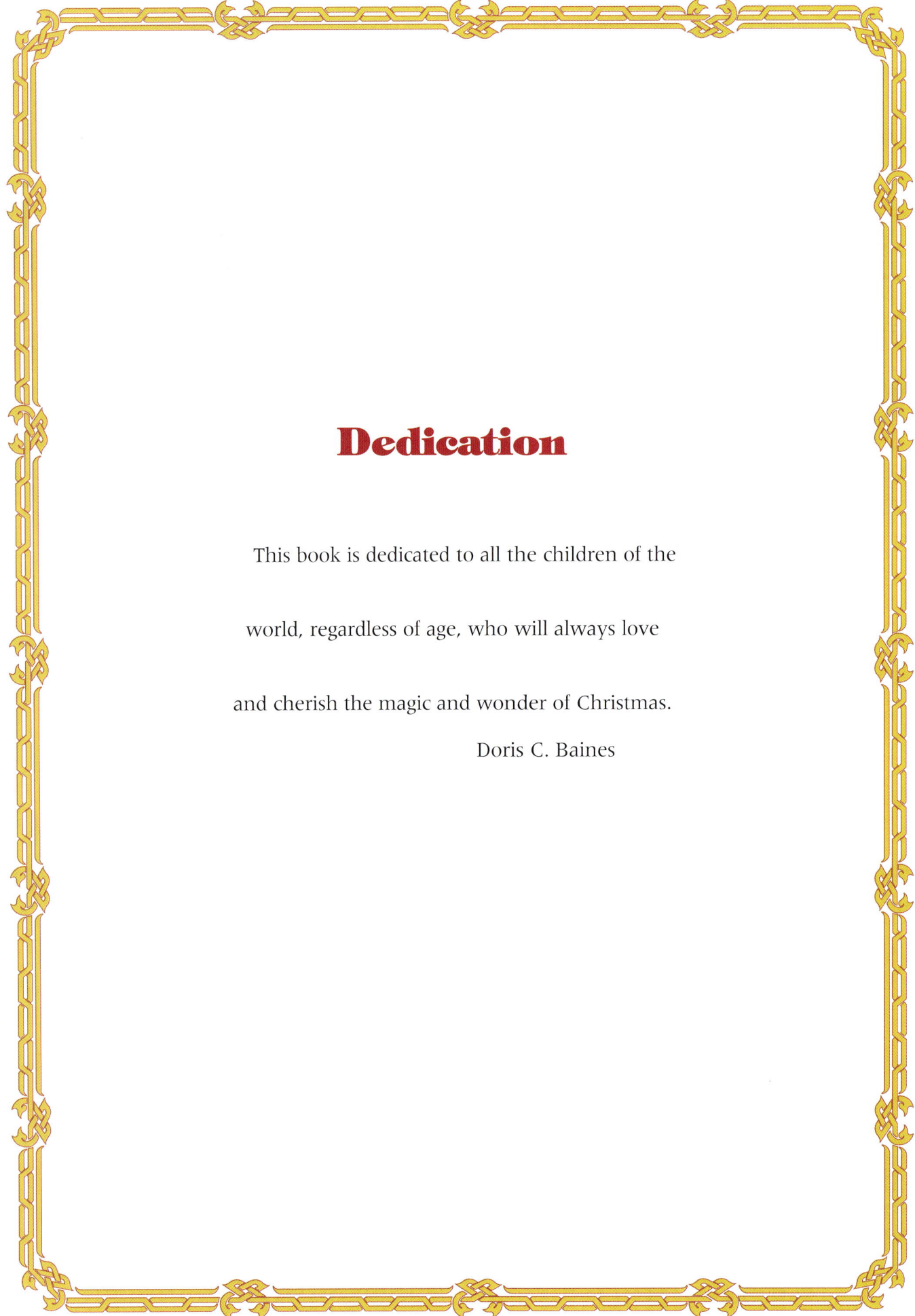

Dedication

This book is dedicated to all the children of the

world, regardless of age, who will always love

and cherish the magic and wonder of Christmas.

            Doris C. Baines

Christmas in the Heart

It is Christmas in the mansion,
Yule-log fires and silken frocks;
It is Christmas in the cottage,
Mother's filling little socks.

It is Christmas on the highway
In the thronging, busy mart;
But the dearest, truest Christmas
Is the Christmas in the heart.

Author Unknown

Table of Contents

Prologue ix

Joy To The World

The Christmas Story 2

Joy to the World 4

Three Wise Men 8

We Three Kings of Orient Are 11

The Legend of the Spider and the Cave 12

Angels We Have Heard On High 14

Away In A Manger

The Legend of St. Francis of Assisi 18

Away in a Manger 20

O Come Let Us Adore Him

O Come Let Us Adore Him 24

The Legend of the Robin 26

The Legend of the Nightingale 28

The Friendly Beasts 30

Star Of Wonder, Star Of Night

The Star 34

Star of Wonder, Star of Night 36

Candles 38

I Heard The Bells On Christmas Day

I Heard the Bells on Christmas Day 44

On The First Day Of Christmas

The Twelve Days of Christmas 48

On the First Day of Christmas 54

The Gift of the Magi, O. Henry 56

Hark! The Herald Angels Sing

Hark! The Herald Angels Sing..........................62
Silent Night, Holy Night 66

Deck The Halls

Deck The Halls 70
Mistletoe 73
The Legend of Mistletoe 74
The Glastonbury Thorn Legend 76
Legend of Poinsettias 78

O Christmas Tree, O Christmas Tree

O Christmas Tree 82
A Christmas Tree Legend 88
The Fir Tree, Hans Christian Andersen 90
Legend of the Fir Tree. 95
The Fire Is So Delightful 96
It's Beginning to Look a Lot Like Christmas 100
The Legend of Icicles 104
The Legend of Tinsel. 106

I'll Be Home For Christmas

The Legend of Christ Child and Yule Dough 110
I'll Be Home for Christmas 112

Santa Claus Is Coming To Town

Santa Claus Is Coming to Town 120
Letters To Santa 125
The Image of Santa. 128
A Visit From Saint Nicholas, Clement C. Moore 129
The Legend of Hanging Stockings.....................130
Yes, Virginia, There Is a Santa Claus. 132

The Legend of Befana, the Ageless Wanderer 134

Baboushka: A Russian Legend 137

Happy Holidays!

Christmas Calenders 140

Advent Calendars 141

Merry Christmas in Different Languages 143

Christmas Cards 144

Christmas Seals 147

The Little Match Girl, Hans Christian Andersen 148

The Nutcracker 150

The Feast of Saint Lucia 152

Christmas Ships 154

Kwanzaa 158

Hanukkah 159

Epilogue 163

Prologue

What Child Is This, Who, laid to rest, on Mary's lap is sleeping?

Whom angels greet with anthems sweet, While shepherds watch are keeping?

This, this is Christ the King, Whom shepherds guard and angels sing:

This, this is Christ the King, the Babe, the Son of Mary.

Christmas is about children. It started with the birth of the Christ Child, and each year we celebrate His birthday by honoring Him and renewing our love and appreciation of our families and friends.

Christmas claims our hearts like no other time of the year. We rejoice in this special time of warmth, closeness and sharing, and we memorialize it as a symbol of what we would like the world to be every day of the year.

Each Christmas brings back memories from our childhood. We remember a particularly grandiose tree, a special gift, a visit from loving grandparents, finding a new and wonderful decoration, as well as the special smells of Christmas for weeks before. Every Christmas we strive to create new memories for our family and savor the wonderful ones we recall from Christmases past.

Perhaps the most precious of all memories is created when we watch the face of a child looking in wonderment at a sparkling, glittering Christmas tree for the first time — or opening that special present that was on the very top of the child's wish list — or that first visit to Santa Claus.

Tradition holds that when the Christmas *crèche* is set up, all the figures are arranged, but the manger remains empty until Christmas morning. When the Christ Child is placed in the crib, it is the moment that truly signifies the meaning of Christmas. This expresses the feeling we have even today — Christmas begins when the child arrives — perhaps the child in all of us.

Christmas comes but once a year, yet lasts a lifetime.

I

Joy to the World

Luke 2:1-20

And it came to pass in those days, that there went out a decree from Caesar Augustus, that all the world should be taxed. (And this taxing was first made when Cyrenius was governor of Syria.)

And all went to be taxed, every one into his own city. And Joseph also went up from Galilee, out of the city of Nazareth, into Judea, unto the city of David, which is called Bethlehem; (because he was of the house and lineage of David:) to be taxed with Mary his espoused wife, being great with child. And so it was, that while they were there, the days were accomplished that she should be delivered.

And she brought forth her first-born son, and wrapped him in swaddling clothes, and laid him in a manger; because there was no room in the inn.

And there were in the same country shepherds abiding in the field, keeping watch over their flock by night.

And, lo, the angel of the Lord came upon them, and the glory of the Lord shone round about them: and they were sore afraid.

And the angel said unto them, Fear not: for, behold I bring you good tidings of great joy, which shall be to all people.

For unto you is born this day in the city of David a Savior, which is Christ the Lord.

And this shall be a sign unto you; Ye shall find the babe wrapped in swaddling clothes lying in a manger.

And suddenly there was with the angel a multitude of the heavenly host, praising God, and saying,

Glory to God in the highest, and on earth, peace, good will toward men.

And it came to pass, as the angels were gone away from them into heaven, the shepherds said one to another, Let us now go even unto Bethlehem, and see this thing which is come to pass, which the Lord has made known to us.

And they came with haste, and found Mary, and Joseph, and the babe lying in a manger.

And when they had seen it, they made known abroad the saying which was told them concerning this child.

And all they that heard it wondered at those things which were told them by the shepherds.

But Mary kept all these things, and pondered them her heart.

And the shepherds returned, glorifying and praising God for all the things that they had heard and seen, as it was told unto them.

"O Holy Night...."

The true date of Christ's birth in Bethlehem is unknown. Early Christians believed that the Nativity took place between 8 and 4 B.C. on the twenty-fifth day of the month, although the exact month is not known. It wasn't until about 320 A.D. that the official date for Christ's birth was designated as December 25 by Julius I, Bishop of Rome. That date was sacred to thousands of fourth century Romans who celebrated *Dies Natalis Invicti Solis*, the Birthday of the Unconquered Sun. This feast honored Mithras, a deity associated with the sun, who was believed to have been born on a rock on December 25. Possibly this remnant of Mithraism may have contributed to choosing December 25 as the Christian holiday. Mithraism originated in Persia, but entered the Roman world in the first century B.C. Emperor Constantine's conversion to Christianity in the fourth century was the act that brought about the ascendance of Christianity to Italy.

Ancient people who were not Christians, Muslim or Jews were known as pagans. They worshiped nature gods who were linked to the rain, sun and agriculture. Many ancient pagan civilizations held mid-winter festivals long before Christ's birth. These festivities celebrated the sun's rebirth and were connected with growing crops, which, of course, were essential to survival. A common belief was that the days grew shorter in December because the sun was leaving or dying, and rituals were created to appease and honor the all-important sun so it would return. These ceremonies were commonly held before December 21. Ultimately, December 25 was chosen as the day of celebration reflecting the importance of the ceremonies to pre-Christian Europe and Asia. In this fashion, the celebration of the sun became the birth date of God's Son.

In Egypt, festivals celebrated the rising of the Nile River which insured that crops would grow each year. More than five thousand years ago, Egyptians observed the celestial path of Sirius, the dog star, and discovered its first annual appearance on the horizon coincided with the Nile's rising. Scholars calculated that the time between one appearance of the star and the next was 365 days. With the adoption of the Dog Star calendar, the original lunar calendar of 360 days was discarded. But the Egyptians were left with five extra days which they added at the end of the year. They devoted these extra days to celebrating with food, drink, special ceremonies, the rededicating of their temples, torchlight processions and the exchange of gifts.

Christmas: Traditions and Legends

The history of mankind cannot be told without noting the holidays, rituals and ceremonies that marked most cultures. As early as 2000 B.C., when the Greeks started occupying the Balkan peninsula, they adopted their newly conquered neighbor's gods and goddesses. One of these was the god of the harvest, Cronus. A celebration in his honor was known as *Kronia* and took place in midsummer after the harvest. In midwinter, the Greeks also had a ceremony to honor Dionysus, their god of wine, in which they lit torches to provide light. The Babylonians and Persians held a midsummer festival known as *Sacaea*, in which owners and slaves exchanged roles. The Teutonic tribes of northern Europe celebrated the winter solstice in honor of Odin. These Germanic people had a great festival called *Yule*, which lasted for twelve days at the end of the year.

One of the best known traditional midwinter celebrations was the one held by the Roman people, known as *Saturnalia*. The Roman god of agriculture was Saturn, and this joyful occasion, held on December 17, honored him. During *Saturnalia*, everyone stopped working, masters and slaves became equals, great feasts and parties were held, and rich and poor alike exchanged gifts of candles, dolls and evergreens. It was an appropriate time for a celebration — food was plentiful, since it was just after the harvest and butchering season. The masters felt slaves should be treated as equals one time of the year as thanks for the work done throughout the year. In some cases, the masters even reversed roles for *Saturnalia*, waiting on their slaves.

A special feast was also held December 25. Pagans decorated their homes with evergreens which, because they kept their color throughout the winter, were believed to hold special powers. Evergreens represented eternal life, and reportedly brought good fortune when exchanged with friends.

At the winter feast, candles were placed in windows, and men and women carrying lighted candles paraded in the streets. Fire was believed to banish darkness and coax the sun to return. People were convinced that unless one offered prayers and performed celebrations to honor the sun, it would not return.

The exchange of gifts, the special ceremonies, evergreens, candles, feasting and a general feeling of celebration, all of course strike a familiar chord since they represent all the elements of our Christmas today. How did these ancient pagan rituals carry over through the hundreds of years and different cultures?

The evolution was fairly natural. When Christianity became established as the state religion of the Roman Empire, church officials attempted to abolish pagan beliefs and festivals. However, since these practices were loved and deeply rooted in people's lives, the church wisely incorporated them to blend with Christian beliefs. Old customs were revised and the focus was directed to honoring Christ as the Light of the World, instead of worshipping the sun and other nature gods.

Since birthdays are always a time for celebration, and new babies are always a cause for jubilation, the Christ Child's birth provided a perfect opportunity to meld these two cultures and strengthen Christianity. Christ became the symbol of life that the sun had been to the pagan worshippers.

The festivities observed in the early days of Christianity were mostly of a religious nature. Three masses were celebrated, beginning at midnight on December 25. This custom was most likely established in the fifth century in Rome, rejoicing that Christ the Saviour was born. Christianity slowly spread throughout Europe, and when it reached England, a special service at midnight commemorated the time of Christ's birth. The English named this service *Cristes maesse* (Christ's Mass), which was finally called Christmas.

The great pagan feasts and parties didn't end with the merging of the two cultures. In fact, in ninth-century England, Alfred the Great declared the twelve days between Christmas and Epiphany, January 6, be set aside for holiday festivities, and that working during those days was illegal. During the Middle Ages, Christmas became England's most popular holiday, celebrated with feasting, drinking, gambling and parading.

Royalty, as well, took an active part in Christmas festivities, and especially delighted in the feasting. Perhaps the most outrageous example was a feast hosted in 1377 by Richard II. He hired two thousand cooks to prepare food for his ten thousand guests. Not to be outdone, in 1415, Henry VI held a "glutton mass celebration" which lasted five days.

All this merriment was too much for the English Puritans, who declared the Christmas observance a "heathen" practice and, in 1647, officially outlawed Christmas celebrations. Puritans went so far as to condemn mince pie, claiming mincemeat had a pagan origin. According to Puritan laws, everyone was required to work Christmas Day; lighting candles and singing carols was strictly forbidden, and churches were closed.

Understandably, these Puritan laws were often ignored. People rebelled against them, and the resulting riots became so common, that some people believed they were part of the Christmas celebration. During one Puritan reign, the English continued to quietly and privately acknowledge Christmas, and when the monarchy was restored to power in 1660, Christmas was reinstated.

In the meantime, the first European settlers who came to America brought their Christmas traditions with them. Since the immigrants came from many different countries, their distinct Christmas customs were continued in their individual homes. Over time, Americans began to adopt each other's traditions and merge them with their own. Though many immigrants clung tenaciously to their old practices, not wanting them to become "Americanized," subsequent generations welcomed other cultures' customs.

The Pilgrims who settled in New England wanted no part of Christmas. Like the Puritans in England, they outlawed the holiday in 1659, and it remained forbidden until 1681. During the time Christmas was outlawed, a fine of five shillings was established for the offense of "observing any such day as Christmas and the like, either by forbearing of labor, feasting, or any other way…" Though the law was repealed in 1681, New Englanders did not embrace Christmas as we know it today until well into the 1800s. For instance, there was no Christmas holiday observed in any New England college in 1847 and classes were held in Boston public schools on Christmas Day as late as 1870.

Though New England did not immediately adopt Christmas, in other parts of the country its celebration flourished. One by one the states of the union made Christmas a legal holiday, beginning with Alabama, in 1836. In 1890, Oklahoma became the last of the forty-eight states or territories to declare December 25 a legal holiday. It is the only national religious holiday so declared by law.

"The most wonderful time of the year.…"

The Three Wise Men

"Now when Jesus was born in Bethlehem of Judea, in the days of Herod the king, behold, there came Wise Men from the east to Jerusalem, saying, 'Where is He that is born King of the Jews? For we have seen His star in the East and are come to worship Him.'

"When Herod the king heard this, he was terrified, and all Jerusalem with him. So assembling the chief priests and professors, he demanded of them where the Messiah would be born. They replied, 'In Bethlehem of Judea;' for it is recorded by the prophet:

"'And you, Bethlehem, in the land of Judah, are by no means least among rulers of Judah; for from you shall come a ruler who will govern my people Israel....'

"Then Herod, having privately interviewed the Magi, ascertained from them the exact time when the star made its appearance. He then sent them to Bethlehem, remarking, 'Go and search diligently for the Child, and when you have found Him, bring me word so I can come and worship Him also.'

"Having listened to the king, they accordingly proceeded on their way, and observed that the star which they had seen at its rising, went before them until arriving, it rested above the place where the Child was. When they observed the star, they rejoiced with very great delight. And having come to the house, they saw the young Child and His mother, Mary, and prostrating themselves, they paid Him homage; and having opened their treasures, they presented Him with gold, frankincense and myrrh, as a tribute...."

There are no names recorded for these Wise Men in the book of Matthew. In fact, it does not even mention that there were three of them. It was suggested that there were three travelers because of the three gifts of gold, frankincense and myrrh presented to the Christ Child. They were likely wise men, but not likely kings. It wasn't until the eighth century that they were given names, physical descriptions and countries of origin. Matthew only states that they followed a star from the East.

Melchoir of Arabia, one of the three, was an old man with gray hair and a long gray beard. Gasper of Tharsis, the youngest, was in his twenties, and ruled in Asia, while

Balthazar of Egypt was middle-aged and dark-skinned. They represented the three races, European, Asian and African, as well as the three stages of life.

The Three Wise Men were also known as the Magi, which means great or learned. Rulers sought their counsel and some believed they had magical powers. In fact, the word magic stems from magi. According to legend, the Wise Men all lived in different countries and had never met. However, each studied the stars nightly and kept charts of their movements. To astrologers like the Magi, the planet's movements, when properly interpreted, predicted coming events. They heard that the Jews were awaiting their Messiah, and learned that according to ancient prophets a new, great star was to appear in the heavens. It was predicted that this star would be unlike any other star ever seen before, and with the star's appearance, a great and long-awaited King was about to be born.

Every night for many years, Melchoir, Gasper and Balthazar each searched the heavens for the special star. One night the Wise Men looked up at the brilliant heavens and knew their search was over. Lighting up the sky was a star brighter and more splendid than they had ever imagined. They knew this was finally the sign they had been waiting for, and each, bearing a gift, and without the knowledge of the other two, started off to follow the star and find the place where the Saviour was born.

By the time they arrived in Jerusalem, word had spread of their journey, and King Herod summoned them to his palace. He, too, had heard rumors about the birth of a child and would not allow any other king in his land.

The Wise Men, unaware of Herod's evil intentions, explained about the star's appearance and how the Child had been born in Bethlehem in Judea, their destination. Herod sent them on, telling them, "Go and search diligently for the Child, and when you have found Him, bring me word so I can come and worship Him also."

The Wise Men traveled toward the star until it seemed to halt in the heavens; then they knew they had found the place where the Baby Jesus was born. They were anxious to worship Him and give Him the gifts they had brought. Melchoir carried a chest of gold, the precious metal symbolizing that Christ was King. Balthazar brought frankincense, a sweet-smelling incense used in temple worship. It was a rare and sacred resin from a tree said to be protected by winged serpents. Burning frankincense was reserved for only the holiest, those who were worshiped and adored. Gasper brought myrrh, a fragrant spice used by the Hebrew people for making medicines and preparing bodies for burial. These gifts ultimately prophesied Jesus' future — gold for a king, frankincense for a high priest, and myrrh for a healer. Perhaps the myrrh was also a prophecy of Jesus' death.

The journey from Jerusalem to Bethlehem supposedly took twelve days, which meant the Wise Men arrived in Bethlehem on January 6. This date, known as Epiphany, Twelfth Night or Three Kings Eve, commemorates their visit and the gifts they brought the Christ Child. This date also established the custom of the Twelve Days of Christmas, and in many Eastern Orthodox countries, January 6 is the date Christmas is celebrated.

According to biblical legend, the Wise Men hurried into the manger, and when they saw the Christ Child, fell to their knees to honor Him, then presented Him with their treasured gifts. The custom of bringing gifts to a newborn child is believed to have started when the Wise Men brought their gifts to the Baby Jesus that first Christmas.

"Bearing gifts we traverse afar...."

We Three Kings Of Orient Are

We three Kings of Orient are,
Bearing gifts we traverse afar,
Field and fountain, moor and mountain,
Following yonder star.

Born a King on Bethlehem's plain
Gold I bring to crown Him again,
King forever, ceasing never
Over us all to reign.

Frankincense to offer have I,
Incense owns a deity high,
Prayer and praising, all men raising
Worship Him, God on high.

Myrrh is mine, its bitter perfume
Breathes a life of gathering gloom;
Sorrow, sighing, bleeding, dying,
Sealed in the stone-cold tomb.

O, star of wonder, star of night...
Guide us to thy perfect light.

The Legend Of The Spider And The Cave

King Herod, King of Judea during the time of Christ's life, was in a terrible rage. He had been told of the birth of a new king, one everyone said would be king of all kings, a savior, someone to be praised and worshiped by all. Herod would not even imagine how a king could be more important than he, so he knew he must do something to destroy this new King, or He would surely take Herod's place. Being a very evil king, Herod came upon a very evil plan.

"I will order all boys under the age of two to be slain," he declared. "That way, there can be no mistake that lets this new King live." And so it was that the order went out into the kingdom.

God, knowing of Herod's monstrous plan, sent an angel to Joseph, father of Jesus, in a dream. The angel warned Joseph, "Arise, and take the Child and His mother and flee into Egypt; and be thou there until I bring thee word; for Herod will seek the young Child, to destroy Him."

Knowing they must obey the angel, Joseph and Mary left immediately for Egypt. The journey was long and perilous, but they knew God would be watching over them.

It was near the end of the first day, and daylight was fading when Joseph said to Mary, "I must find a place for us to spend the night." He spotted a cave nearby and led Mary and the Babe into it. Just as they slipped inside, one of Herod's soldiers appeared in the distance.

A little spider, who lived near the cave, had seen Mary and Joseph take the Christ Child into the cave, and heard the pounding hooves of King Herod's approaching soldiers. As quickly as his little legs could move, the spider spun a web up and down, around and around, until it covered the entrance to the cave. He had never worked so hard or so fast.

As soon as the spider had spun the very last strand, the soldiers appeared. The little spider's heart was pounding so loudly, he thought surely the soldiers would hear it. Just as they seemed ready to burst in and search the cave, the captain noticed the web.

"There cannot possibly be anyone in that cave," he told his men, "for if anyone had gone in, the spider's web would certainly be broken. Come, let us go on."

The little spider was so proud and pleased, he thought he would explode. He knew the Holy Family was safe now and could continue on their journey to Egypt in peace. He also knew that his special gift to the Babe would never be forgotten.

Next time you see a spider, remember the one who saved the Baby Jesus from King Herod's soldiers.

Angels We Have Heard On High

When the angel Clarence finally earns his wings in the movie, *It's a Wonderful Life,* everything seems to be right with the world. Jimmy Stewart's character who was poised to jump off the bridge, changes his mind, the town rallies around him and his family, and Clarence gets to return to heaven, a proud and successful guardian angel.

Angels have always been special, and this popular film, shown each year, has become the definitive Christmas movie. Clarence doesn't match our image of the typical angel, but he grabs our heartstrings in a way that makes us certain angels are as important in heaven as Clarence was to the movie family.

God chose Gabriel, another very important angel, to tell Mary of the upcoming birth of Christ. Mary was betrothed to Joseph, and, when Gabriel appeared, he told her, "The Lord is with you and has greatly blessed you. You have received a gift from God. You shall conceive and give birth to a Son; and you shall give Him the name of Jesus."

"While shepherds watched their flocks by night
   All seated on the ground,
   The angel of the Lord came down
   And glory shone around."

Gabriel also appeared to the shepherds the night Jesus was born. They were tending their sheep in the countryside outside Bethlehem when a brilliant light shone in the sky. The shepherds were frightened by the blinding light, but Gabriel said to them,

"Fear not: for behold, I bring you good tidings of great joy, which shall be to all people. For unto you is born this day, in the city of David, a Saviour, which is Christ the Lord. And this shall be a sign unto you: ye shall find the Babe wrapped in swaddling clothes, lying in a manger."

And then, the sky filled with angels, who sang with Gabriel, "Glory to God in the highest, peace on earth, and good will to men."

A few days later, an angel of the Lord appeared to Joseph in a dream and told him to take Mary and the Christ Child and flee to Egypt. The evil king Herod had heard of the birth, and ordered all baby boys under the age of two to be killed. Joseph fled with Mary and the Babe to Egypt and safety.

In some European countries, an angel is the one who brings Christmas gifts to children. Children in South America believe their letters to the "Little Jesus" which contain their Christmas lists are taken to heaven by angels. In Hungary, children believe that on Christmas Eve, one of God's angels decorates the tree as well as brings the presents. It is said the angel then visits each sleeping child, smiling and blessing him or her before going on the next house.

For many of us, an angel is a must for the top of our Christmas tree — nothing else will do. We also have special angel decorations and tree ornaments and, all little girls dream of being an angel in the school or church Christmas pageant. Angels get to wear wings and pretty, long robes, and a halo that is all shiny.

Christmas songs are often about angels, such as *The First Noel, It Came Upon a Midnight Clear; O, Come All ye Faithful*, and of course, *Hark. The Herald Angels Sing*. Maybe you can remember more.

God chose angels to tell the birth of the Christ Child. All these carols help retell the story, and each year remind us of the important message they carry.

Hark! The herald angels sing, glory to the Newborn King.

Clarence was right to be so proud when he earned his wings.

"O hear the angel voices...."

II

Away in a Manger

The Legend Of St. Francis Of Assisi

Francis of Assisi was an Italian nobleman who was born in 1182 or 1183. His childhood was carefree and comfortable. In his twenties, Francis denounced his noble lifestyle and dedicated himself to serving God. One legend claims that a crucifix spoke to him, urging him to "go repair my house, which is falling in ruin." Francis believed this meant God wanted him to repair and restore churches, and he begged in the streets for money for these restoration projects. He also founded the Franciscans, a religious order which served the poor, and became known as the "Little Brother of Mankind."

Francis began preaching throughout the countryside, wherever people would listen, and soon developed a great reputation and following. He was a gentle man with a burning passion to share his devotion to God with his fellow men. In the thirteenth century, very few people could read, and for those with this ability, the selection of books was limited. Francis' greatest desire was to simplify the story of Christ, in contrast to the ornate representations in his time, and to show people the humble beginnings of Christ so they could relate to the story. He searched his soul for a way to do this.

A famous account describes Francis walking toward the village of Greccio, where he was to speak. Along the way he noticed shepherds sleeping in the fields, reminding him of the shepherds who visited the Christ Child the night He was born in Bethlehem. Francis remembered the image of the manger where the Baby Jesus lay in a feedbox filled with hay, surrounded by Joseph, Mary, the animals, shepherds and the Wise Men. Francis remembered seeing this humble scene elaborately recreated in churches he had visited. In one nativity pageant, the Christ Child lay in an ornate hand-carved cradle, and Joseph and Mary were clothed in rich robes of silk and brocade. The Magi, too, wore elaborate gold and silver robes encrusted with jewels. These nativity scenes bore little resemblance to the modest surroundings in Bethlehem where Jesus was born.

It was Christmas Eve morning, and Francis wanted to deliver a special message at his service that evening. He knew the story of Christ's birth had been studied by leaders of the church, but he wanted ordinary people to understand that God's Son was born in a lowly stable, and thus had a simple beginning like many of them. The striking image of the stable in Bethlehem nagged at him, until suddenly the answer came to him. If the people could actually *see* a realistic depiction of what it had been like that first Christmas Eve so many years ago, maybe it would help them understand the full meaning of Christ's birth.

The people of Greccio had been told the services would be held in a nearby cave. Though many questioned this choice, they arrived early. Aware of St. Francis' reputation, they had traveled many miles to hear him speak.

No one was prepared for the vision that met them when they approached the cave. St. Francis had completely re-created the nativity scene, including a manger filled with straw, and a live ox and ass. Village people acted the roles of Joseph, Mary and the shepherds, and a carved figure of Jesus lay in the manger.

Shouts of joy and delight were heard throughout the countryside, and the candles the worshippers carried seemed to light up the sky with their glow. As Francis told the simple and inspiring story of the birth of the Christ Child, the small village became a new Bethlehem. Then he asked the children to join him in singing what some believe were the first Christmas carols. Everyone who attended that Christmas service in the cave outside Greccio would always remember the simpler meaning of Christmas. It was through St. Francis' vision the original Christmas Eve was born again.

Away In A Manger

"A little child, a shining star
A stable crude, the door ajar
Yet in that place, so plain, forlorn
The hope of all the world was born."

– Anonymous

The nativity scene is one of the most recognized symbols of Christmas throughout the world. Originally seen only in churches, nativities today are part of many home and outdoor decorations. Nativity scenes are sometimes simple, made by schoolchildren out of cardboard, depicting only the Holy Family. Others contain life-sized figures wearing elaborate clothing, and include the shepherds, animals, and the Wise Men. Some churches present a live re-enactment in a Christmas pageant. Whatever form the nativity takes, it almost always carries a universal message of reverence and love.

Word of St. Francis' manger scene spread quickly. Those who attended the service in the cave were so overwhelmed, they wanted to share this phenomenon. Soon scenes similar to the re-enactment in Greccio began to appear in countries throughout Europe. At first only live presentations were performed. Soon, however, miniature wooden figures of the animals, the Wise Men, and the Holy Family became part of many families' Christmas displays.

The Italian word for manger is *presepio*; in France, the cradle is a *crèche*; the German word for crib is *krippe*. Spanish-speaking nations have their *naciemento*. The Morovians, a small Protestant group from Germany who founded the town of Bethlehem, Pennsylvania, called their crib the *putz* (from the German word *putzen* — to decorate). The people of each country adapted the nativity scene to their own culture, the figures sometimes resembling their creators more than the Holy Family.

The re-enactment of the nativity scene during Christmas became especially popular in Italy, perhaps because of the influence of St. Francis. At first, most of the re-creations were fairly simple, like the Christmas Eve in Greccio. But in Naples during the eighteenth century, nativities became more and more elaborate; indeed, many were works of art. Leading families competed for the most beautiful and detailed presentations at holiday gatherings. Famous painters of the time painted the nativity scene while sculptors chose it as their subject throughout history. These often romantic figures were a long way from the manger in which the Baby Jesus was born in a feedbox filled with hay. Frequently the robes worn by the Magi were of exquisite material richly embroidered with jewels, and the crib was magnificently carved out of rare wood. Some nativity scenes were so large they filled an entire room.

Perhaps the best-loved ritual in Rome is held at midnight Christmas Eve in the Church of Santa Maria in Aracoeli which is built on the site of the ancient Roman capital. *Ara Coeli* means "altar of the heavens," and according to legend, the Emperor Augustus, having heard rumors that he was to be honored as a god, perceived a vision and heard a voice which told him, "This is the altar of the Son of God," and immediately raised an altar on the site, the *Ara Coeli*. At the midnight Christmas Eve service, a wooden statue of the Christ Child (said to have been carved from an olive tree in the Garden of Gethsemene) is brought from a private chapel to a throne near the high altar. Upon intonation of the "Gloria," a veil is removed and the statue is taken to a Nativity Crib in the left side nave. From this perch on the wooden manger, the *Santo Bambino* receives tributes from the children of Rome. A temporary platform is constructed each year for the children to recite prayers, poems and requests. The statue of the Holy Child remains in this place of honor until Epiphany, when after a benediction of the city and its people, it is returned to the chapel.

In France, to create a realistic atmosphere, children go into the woods and gather rocks, greenery and moss to place around the *crèche*. Painted clay figures called santons are placed in the *crèche* to represent the Biblical characters and village inhabitants.

To the German people, the *krippe* has always been the heart of Christmas. It is their most treasured symbol, with most families having their own *krippe* handed down from generation to generation. Christmas markets — *Christkindlmarkte* — have existed for hundreds of years in Germany, and each year families buy pieces at these markets to add to their *krippe*. Some expanded *krippen* include complete villages with trees, buildings, cows and flocks of sheep.

The *naciemento* in Spain contains all the traditional figures, but a few distinctly Spanish ones are also featured. A Spanish bull watches over Christ from a nearby stall, and bullfighters are frequently added to the setting. A small stream always appears as a place where women kneel as they tend to the family laundry. Children dance and sing nativity songs around the altar, as the scenes are frequently set up in public squares.

In the Church of the Nativity in Bethlehem, a statue of the Christ Child is brought to the altar after the first Mass. The statue is then carried in procession to a crypt where it is laid on a silver star marking the spot believed to be the actual site of Jesus' birth. The Gospel of Saint Luke is sung, and upon hearing the words, "...she laid Him in a manger," the statue is lifted from the floor and placed in a rock-hewn crib next to the star.

One year in the 1960s at the annual Festival of Trees on Waikiki Beach in Honolulu, Hawaii, the *crèche* was fashioned from coconut husks and pandanus pine leaves. The Three Kings wore fresh orchid leis and their gifts to the Christ Child were gem-sprinkled pineapples and talking mynah birds.

Christmas pageants featuring the nativity scene take place all over America today. In Cleveland's Trinity Episcopal Cathedral, over one hundred performers dress as participants in the original nativity. They are accompanied by a choir of over two hundred voices. In 1993, the International *Crèche* Festival was founded in Bellingham, Washington. The day after Thanksgiving, local businesses placed nativity-scene displays in their windows. In its second year, there were more than fifty entries from thirty-four countries. Each *crèche* depicts the Christmas story as envisioned by artisans from all around the world. The unique qualities of each is illustrated by the varying materials, textures and colors. Some scenes show a cradle in a cave; others display a hammock in a jungle tree. The *crèche* may be carved out of wood, or made of porcelain, corn husks, glass, crêpe paper or cattails. Each reflects the flavor of the native country of the artist but tells the same Christmas story which lets the viewer enjoy the wondrous diversity of the world in which we live.

Each year the Metropolitan Museum of Art in New York exhibits a giant blue spruce featuring a collection of eighteenth-century Neapolitan angels and cherubs on its branches, and a baroque *crèche* nested at its base. More than two hundred eighteenth-century Neapolitan *crèche* figures were presented to the museum in 1964 and have been on display each Christmas since. Each figure is a work of art, ranging from six to twenty inches in height. Special tree-lighting ceremonies are held throughout the season, and Christmas concerts are performed in front of the magnificent tree.

The nativity scene best symbolizes the true religious spirit of Christmas — from the smallest cardboard stable made by children, to the largest, most elaborate exhibit. The scene that shows the humble beginnings of Jesus clearly signifies what Christmas means to Christians all over the world.

"The Little Lord Jesus lay down
His sweet head...."

III

O Come Let Us Adore Him

It is said the night the Christ Child was born was the darkest night ever. At the moment of Jesus' birth, a great light spread across the sky which suddenly filled with angels. Green leaves sprouted on the dead branches of trees, blossoms and berries covered barren vines, flowers sprang out of the ground, and animals spoke.

In some European countries, it is still believed that at midnight on Christmas Eve, animals are given the power of speech to announce the birthday of Christ. It is rumored that it is dangerous to listen to them speak, and stories warn of dire misfortune to those who try.

Of course the animals were in the manger when Jesus was born, sharing their lowly stable with Him. Because they showed their adoration by falling on their knees at midnight on Christmas Eve, animals have always played a special part in the Christmas celebration. Even today, animals are depicted hovering protectively over Christ in many nativity scenes.

It was bitter cold in the manger, and the Christ Child, like all newborns, needed to be kept warm. As the animals and birds in the manger watched, the cow warmed the Little Babe with her breath and did not eat her hay so Mary could cushion the cradle. Mary blessed the creature for her kindness and, since then, the cow has had the sweetest breath of all animals. The wren brought moss and feathers to make a coverlet. The lamb gave his wool to line the cradle, and the doves cooed the Baby Jesus to sleep. All the animals knelt in adoration and whispered, "Let us worship Him together."

In some foreign countries today, an honored tradition is still observed, where all animals, birds, and even fish are safe from human predators on Christmas Eve. Livestock are given extra or special portions of food on Christmas, often from the tables of their masters.

Old tales recount people walking into the woods on Christmas Day and finding all animals at peace with one another — joined in harmony for one day — predator and prey. Some people believe that the animals speak among themselves on Christmas Day and can even foretell the future.

At Christmas we still honor the farm animals in decorations and nativity scenes, but another animal has become a popular part of our Christmas traditions. A relative newcomer who wasn't in the manger with the ox, sheep or donkey. In fact, this animal wasn't even part of Christmas until 1949. It's the most famous reindeer of all — *Rudolph*.

This beloved story about a red-nose reindeer first touched the hearts of children all over America in 1939. The Depression had just ended and, as a promotion, Montgomery Ward decided to have their store Santas give gifts to the children who came to visit them. Robert May, an employee, wrote a little story about a magical reindeer named Rudolph. The store gave away 2,400,000 copies of the book in 1939, and 3,600,000 when the promotion was used again in 1946. Then Montgomery Ward decided they no longer wanted to use the story and returned the copyright to the author. In 1949, May sent the story to Johnny Marks, a songwriter, who not only wrote the musical version, but arranged for it to be recorded by Gene Autry. The song rose to the top of the *Hit Parade* that year, and Rudolph has been part of America's Christmas tradition ever since.

Maybe those who believe animals can talk on Christmas Eve are right. After all, the reindeer and Santa all talked to Rudolph — at least the other reindeer "laughed and called him names," and Santa asked Rudolph to guide his sleigh through the cloudy weather. No one knows if Rudolph answered, but it's a pretty good bet he understood.

O Come Let Us Adore Him

"You'll go down in history...."

The Legend Of The Robin

It was late on the night the Christ Child was born. The stable was freezing, and the fire that warmed the Holy Family dwindled until it was barely smoldering. Joseph and Mary were asleep, but the Little Babe had awakened, shivering from the cold and He began to cry.

Just then, a little bird flew into the manger to escape the bitter cold and seek warmth inside the stable. As soon as he saw the Christ Child trembling and crying, he forgot how cold he was and thought, "I must do something or the Baby Jesus will freeze to death."

He was not a pretty bird. In fact, the little bird was just a plain, dull gray color. No brightly colored or shiny feathers covered him. But he knew that his appearance would not matter if he could save the Babe from the cold.

Perching on a log near the coals, the little gray bird began to flap his wings as hard as he could. Nothing happened except that the coals got dimmer and dimmer. Then the little bird realized he had to fly *over* the fire so his wings could fan the coals into flames.

The tiny bird started flying back and forth over the coals, flapping his wings with all his might. Back and forth, back and forth until his wings felt as though they would fall right off his little back. Still, the flames would not come, and the Christ Child's crying became louder and louder.

"Oh, I am so tired. I must rest for just a minute," thought the little bird as he perched on the log again. "Then I will try *one* more time, and this time I will fly and flap like no other bird has ever done before!"

After resting just a bit, the little bird gathered up his last *tiny* bit of strength and started flying over the embers, flapping his very best flap. Suddenly, the coals burst into flames and started to burn — in fact, the flames lit up the entire manger.

The little bird was *so* excited, he didn't realize he had flown so close to the flames that his breast was burned. It was bright red, as red as the flames, and it started to throb with pain. Yet, it barely mattered, for the fire was burning brightly, and the Baby Jesus was warm again and stopped crying.

And then Mary awakened and understood the little bird's valiant efforts. She picked him up and soothed his scorched breast with her soft hands until all the pain disappeared.

"You are *most* brave, little bird," she told him, "and because of your bravery, you shall keep your pretty red breast, which no other bird shall have."

The little bird looked at his beautiful new bright, red breast and knew he was indeed special and that *no one* would ever again mistake him for just a dull gray bird. Ever since, this bird has been called the *robin redbreast*.

The Legend Of The Nightingale

In the stable in Bethlehem, the tiny Baby Jesus was crying, and His mother, Mary, could not quiet Him. She was exhausted from their long journey, and from all the excitement after the Christ Child was born. So many people had come to worship and honor her new Son, it was not surprising the Little Babe was fussing.

"I will sing a lullaby and hold and rock Him," she thought, "and then He will surely be comforted enough to sleep."

In a soft, sweet voice, Mary sang two of her favorite lullabies, remembered and loved from her childhood. As she sang, she rocked the Christ Child, holding Him close to her heart. Still, the Little Babe cried.

Meanwhile, perched on the roof of the manger, a nightingale had been listening carefully to her singing. He, too, was upset that the Little Infant was still crying.

"I must help quiet the Christ Child," he thought, and flew down from his perch landing on Mary's shoulder. Near tears from being so tired and upset, Mary did not even notice the little bird on her shoulder.

When Mary started to sing another lullaby, her voice quivered and she could barely be heard. And then, the nightingale joined her. Puffing up proudly, he began to sing a clear, sweet tune. In fact, he was singing so sweetly, Mary stopped her own singing to listen. And then a miraculous thing happened. Baby Jesus became calm in Mary's arms, looked up at the nightingale, and smiled. The little bird's voice became sweeter and sweeter, and he thought he would surely burst with pride. And finally, the Infant slept quietly in His mother's arms.

Mary laid the Babe gently in the cradle, then turned to the nightingale. "Oh, that was such a lovely lullaby. Thank you for coming here and quieting the Baby Jesus. You have sung Him to sleep when I could not. Because you sang *so* beautifully, I will make your voice the sweetest of all the birds who sing."

And, to this day, the nightingale, which means "night singer," has been known for his varied and melodious singing, heard especially at night. It is said when nightingales sing, the trees, the flowers, and even the other birds stop to listen.

The Friendly

Jesus our brother, strong and good
Was humbly born in a stable rude,
And the friendly beasts around Him stood
Jesus our brother, strong and good.

"I," said the donkey, shaggy and brown,
"I carried His mother up hill and down,
I carried her safely to Bethlehem town;
I," said the donkey, shaggy and brown.

"I," said the cow, all white and red,
"I gave Him my manger for His bed,
I gave Him my hay to pillow His head,
"I," said the cow, all white and red.

"I," said the sheep, with curly horn,
"I gave Him my wool for His blanket warm,
He wore my coat on Christmas morn;
"I," said the sheep, with curly horn.

"I," said the dove, from his rafters high,
"Cooed Him to sleep, my mate and I;
We cooed Him to sleep, my mate and I;
"I," said the dove, from his rafters high.

And every beast, by some good spell,
In the stable dark was glad to tell,
Of the gift he gave Immanuel,
Of the gift he gave Immanuel.

– Author Unknown

Beasts

An old legend tells of the animals who spread the message of the Christ Child's birth.

The cock was the first to proclaim the news, flying to a large perch and crowing loudly, "Christ is born."

The raven was excited by this wonderful news and croaked, "When?"

The rook proudly answered, "This night."

The ox was listening. "Where?" he asked.

The sheep knew and proclaimed, "In Bethlehem."

The ass could wait no longer. "Let us go," he brayed.

The bees led the way, humming a lovely carol.

IV

Star of Wonder
Star of Night

The Star

There's a star in the East
On Christmas morn
Rise up, shepherd, and follow.
It'll lead to the place
Where the Saviour's born
Rise up, shepherd, and follow.
If you take good heed
To the angel's words and
Rise up, shepherd, and follow.
You'll forget your flocks,
You'll forget your herds,
Rise up, shepherd, and follow.
Leave your sheep, leave your lambs,
Rise up, shepherd, and follow.
Leave your ewes, leave your rams,
Rise up, shepherd, and follow.
Follow the Star of Bethlehem,
Rise up, shepherd, and follow.

– Author Unknown

Star Of Wonder Star Of Night

"Wasn't that a mighty day
When Jesus Christ was born
A star shone in the east
A star shone in the east
A star shone in the east
When Jesus Christ was born."

– Author Unknown

The Three Wise Men studied the stars nightly. They noted the constellations in the night sky and watched their movements. One winter night they knew the star that blazed overhead was the one they had been waiting for, a sign that a great King was about to be born. This star shone bigger, brighter, more wondrous than any star they had ever seen and they knew they must follow it. Since they were traveling in a strange land and were not sure of the way, they stopped in Jerusalem and asked King Herod, "…Where is He who has been born King of the Jews? For we have seen His star in the East, and have come to worship Him."

In the time just before Christ's birth, stars were worshiped as signs of God's work, and it was a truly special star that guided the Wise Men to the spot where Jesus was born. According to Saint Matthew, 2: 9,10, "…and lo, the star, which they saw in the east, went before them, till it came and stood over where the Child was. When they saw the star, they rejoiced with exceeding great joy."

Because of the star's role in leading the Wise Men to Jerusalem during Christmas, stars are still prominently featured in our churches and homes. We place them at the top of our Christmas trees, and they shine above the nativity scenes. We make star-shaped cookies and decorations, and we send Christmas cards and use Christmas wrappings with stars printed on them. A lighted star at the top of a church, its rays of light shimmering, is a sight so magnificent you can't help but liken it to the star that led the Wise Men.

At Christmas we sing songs about stars. One of the most familiar is, "Star of wonder, star of night / Guide us to thy perfect light."

Another favorite Christmas carol is, "O holy night / The stars are brightly shining / It is the night of the dear Saviour's birth."

Stars have special significance in other countries. In Poland, the Star of Bethlehem is very important. No one can celebrate the holiday on Christmas Eve until the sighting of the first star, which represents the Star of Bethlehem. That sighting signals the end of Advent and fasting and the beginning of their Festival of the Star, *vigilia* (*wilia*). This Christmas Eve feast consists of thirteen courses, one for Jesus and one for each of His disciples.

In Romania, children carry six-pointed revolving star lanterns through the streets, stopping at each door to sing carols about the star that shone over Bethlehem. In the Philippines, *parols,* which are star lanterns, are displayed in front of homes and shops. Many communities have a contest to determine the most beautiful or largest *parol*. Families hand down their design for making *parols*, which are created from bamboo frames covered with colored paper and trimmed in lace, tassels and pom-poms.

Some of the descendants of Russian settlers in Alaska include a Christmas celebration called "Carrying the Star." Beginning January 7, which is the Russian Orthodox Christmas, and continuing for three days, men, women, and children of Kodiak move through the streets carrying tinsel and ribbon-trimmed wheels. The wheel-stars are umbrella-sized and may have a center decoration featuring the nativity. Each year, families restore their star, and parts of several are over 100 years old. The star-carriers, representing the angels who announced Christ's birth, often sing carols and are invited into the homes for refreshments.

Perhaps the city that best portrays the significance of stars in America is the self-proclaimed "Christmas City," Bethlehem, Pennsylvania. On top of South Mountain, there is a ninety-foot electric star overlooking the city. The star used to be lit only during the month of December, but it was so popular it now shines throughout the year. This Star of Bethlehem can be seen for twenty miles and serves as a welcome to all who visit the area. The official seal of the city is the Star of Bethlehem — its five points representing religion, music, industry, recreation and education.

The people in Palmer Lake, Colorado, also have a Star of Bethlehem, which is 500 feet wide and displayed on a mountainside, where it is visible for twenty miles. The Palmer Lake Christmas Star dates back to 1934, when the entire community took part in building it on property donated to the city. The fire department of Palmer Lake maintains the star, which, with the exception of the World War II years, has been lit every December since 1934. The people of Palmer Lake lighted the star when the Iran hostages were released and again at the end of Desert Storm. It is their wish that those who see it will find hope, inspiration and good will toward men all year long, not just at Christmas.

For years, astronomers have studied the stars, the moon and the planets. Their reasons for studying are far different from the prophecy that led the Wise Men to a humble manger on that winter night so long ago. But, if that special star could help the Wise Men find Jesus, maybe it helps Santa Claus find your house each Christmas Eve.

"O morning stars together proclaim the holy birth...."

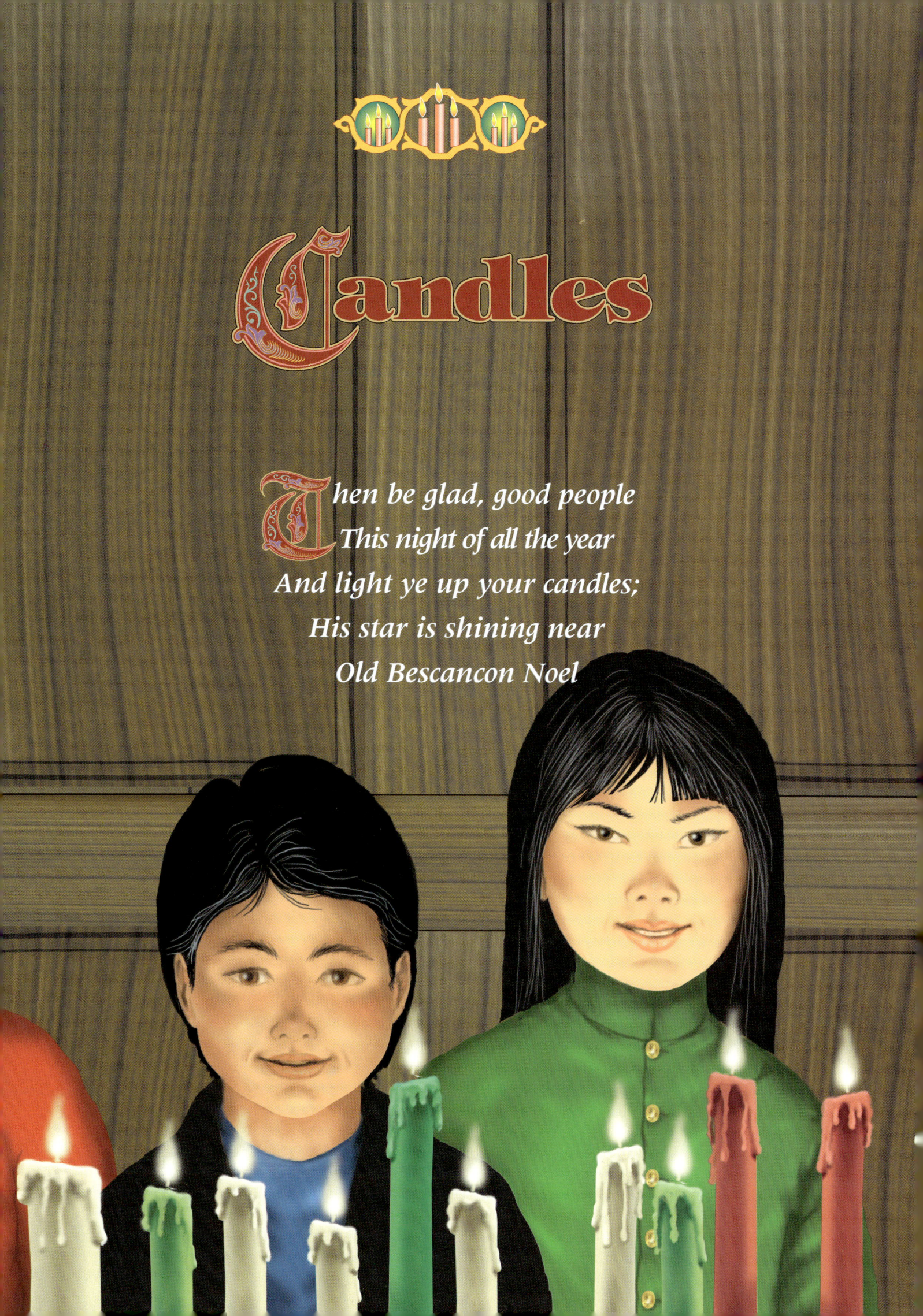

Candles

Then be glad, good people
This night of all the year
And light ye up your candles;
His star is shining near
Old Bescancon Noel

Candles

To ancient Romans, candles lit in the heart of winter represented darkness ending and the light of spring forthcoming. Christians believed candles represented Christ, the Light of the World. Historians believe that candles may have been the first of the pagan symbols to be adopted by Christians.

During the festival of *Saturnalia,* when everyone was considered equal, candles were a proper gift for a lower-ranking person to give to a higher-ranking person. Even the poorest families had at least one candle during the holiday season. In medieval Europe, a very large candle, called the Christmas candle, was burned until the Twelfth Night, in remembrance of the arrival of the Wise Men to Bethlehem.

It was also a custom to put lighted candles in windows of homes in case the Christ Child needed guidance through the darkness. In Victorian times, candles were placed in windows during the Twelve Days of Christmas to indicate welcome to any passerby needing shelter and food.

Certain beliefs were attached to candles. The wax was said to represent Christ's body, the wick His soul, and the flame His divine nature. Some people believed the flames from the burning candles frightened away evil spirits. Norwegians believed if candles were allowed to burn out on Christmas Eve, they would be cursed with bad luck the following year.

During *Saturnalia,* Romans fastened candles to trees growing outdoors. The custom of lighting candles on trees indoors started in Germany and is one of many customs that found its way to America. Candles were wired to tree branches and, though they were beautiful, they presented a tremendous fire hazard. Some families lit the candles just once for the children. Even then, an adult was usually standing by with a bucket of water. Fire departments grew weary of being called out during Christmas, and the invention of electric lights was especially welcome to firemen.

Originally, candles were made from tallow, a fat extracted from animals. Since tallow was plentiful, candles were affordable. Wax candles were preferred, as the wax from virgin bees was said to represent Mary's purity. Eventually wax candles became less expensive and more common.

The four Sundays prior to Christmas are known as Advent. Many Christians celebrate Advent with a wreath that holds candles. On the first Sunday of Advent, one candle is lit, then the second, third and fourth on each successive Sunday. Often, an additional, larger candle is lit on Christmas Eve, with all five burning candles representing the light Christ brought into the world.

Candlemas Day, February 2, is the day Roman and Greek Catholic churches bless candles for the year. These candles are used in all church functions. It is a custom in some countries to keep remains of blessed candles to protect one from harm in the coming year.

In the southwestern United States, an old Spanish custom is observed. Candles are placed in paper bags, partly filled with sand, then set on porches or edges of roofs to welcome carolers or to cheer passersby. Throughout the Southwest, entire neighborhoods are decorated with these candles. In

Phoenix, Arizona, the Desert Botanical Garden features over seventy-five hundred of these candles, called *luminarias,* glowing in the dark each night for three nights. They are also popular in New Mexico and Texas, especially in San Antonio, where hundreds line the banks of River Walk.

People all over the world put candles in their windows on Christmas Eve. They symbolize that a light is always a welcome guide to weary travelers just as the star guided the Wise Men to Bethlehem. In an early Christmas legend, the Holy Child wanders the earth on Christmas Eve, looking for a place to stay. Thus no traveler can be turned away on Christmas Eve in case the Christ Child might come by. In some areas of Germany, children leave lighted candles in the window so the Christ Child can find their house to leave gifts.

The people of Williamsburg, Virginia, a restored historical village, celebrate each year with their "Grand Illumination." All the homes, shops, and the Governor's Palace blaze with lighted candles in the windows from early December to early January. Carolers stroll from house to house through walkways glowing with candlelight.

Many, many years ago, candles were the only way you could light your home. Though candles have been replaced by electric lights in modern times, their presence, especially at Christmas, signifies the message of the season. Carolers carry candles as they stroll singing throughout the neighborhood. Lighted candles fill homes and church windows during the holiday season, and candlelight services are held Christmas Eve in churches all over the world. Each year Christmas candles remind us that we are celebrating the birth of He who became the Light of the World.

"And light ye up your candles...."

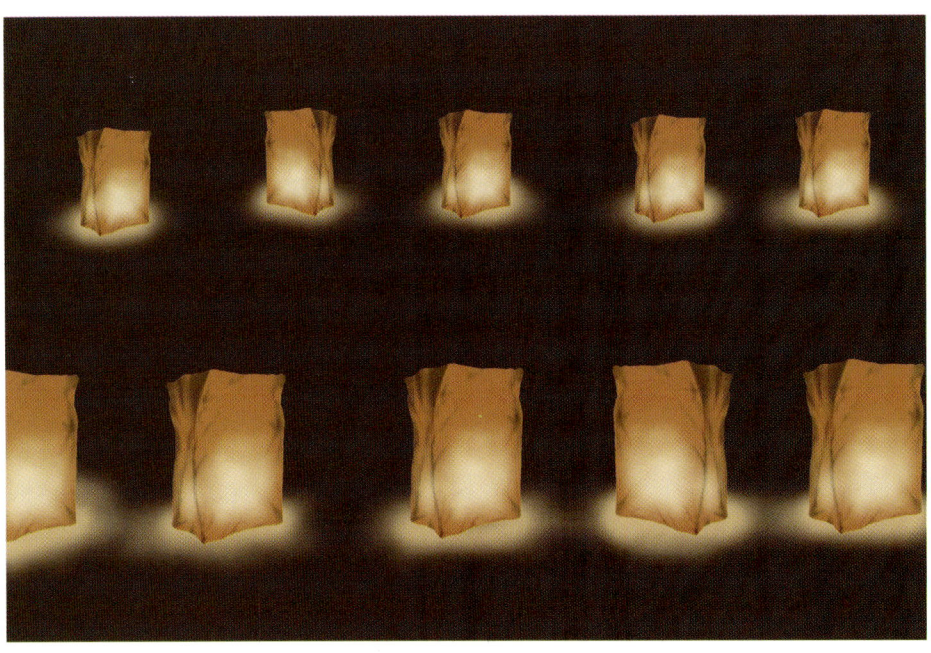

Doris Baines

V

I Heard the Bells on Christmas Day

I Heard The Bells On Christmas Day

At midnight when Jesus was born, bells rang out to tell the world of His birth. Those were the days long before radio or television, and ringing bells called people to church or relayed news of special occasions such as a victory in war or the birth of a king. Ever since, during the Christmas season, church bells chime to remind us of the birthday of the King of Kings.

In medieval times, an interesting custom was practiced in England, Ireland and Scotland. One hour before midnight on Christmas Eve, the big bell in the church steeple began a slow, solemn tolling. It was a mournful sound, as if tolling for a funeral. Then, at midnight, the bells suddenly rang out in a joyous peal. According to legend, this signified that Satan died when Christ was born. In parts of Ireland, the village church bell is still rung from eleven o'clock to midnight on Christmas Eve. The custom is called "the devil's funeral."

Many years ago, bells were believed to be endowed with unique powers and they were rung to ward off storms, chase away enemies and put out fires. Some cultures believed that bells possessed almost human characteristics and dedicated them in a baptismal type of ceremony before they were installed in the steeple. Medieval people believed bells could terrify evil spirits, and that witches and goblins were afraid of bells.

There are many legends about bells. One legend tells of a village in England, where the deeply religious townsfolk gathered at the church each Christmas Eve. The church bells were a great source of pride to the villagers, since they had worked hard to buy them in a far-off city. Each Christmas, they rang the bells and proclaimed the glad tidings of the birth of the Christ Child in a glorious celebration that everyone looked forward to and participated in. However, a calamity occurred when an earthquake buried the church and all its bells. Nonetheless, it is said that if you believe in Christ, you can travel to the church site on Christmas Eve, and if you put your head to the ground, you can still hear the bells ringing. They have a happy ring just as they had for the people in the village years ago. They tell the message, "Christ is born."

In Spain, people tell the story of an old woman who insisted she heard bells under a church floor. She was so determined, the authorities finally dug up the floor to discover a large bell and a statue of the Virgin Mary buried there.

During the Puritan era in England, when people were forbidden to celebrate Christmas, a town crier traveled the towns ringing a shrill-sounding hand bell to remind everyone that celebrating was not allowed. There is a bit of irony here, since bells, which had always been a part of the Christmas tradition, were used to warn people not to celebrate.

During this same period in England, the English declared bells evil and ordered them dismantled from their towns and sold. There is a legend of a ship carrying bells away from England when it sank. Inhabitants of a nearby village claim that on Christmas Eve you can hear the bells ringing from the depths of the sea where the ship went down. These stories no doubt account for the belief that any church bells destroyed or broken will still ring on Christmas Eve.

The familiar Christmas carol, *I Heard the Bells on Christmas Day,* was originally a poem written by Henry Wadsworth Longfellow on Christmas Eve in 1863, six months after the Battle of Gettysburg, at the height of the Civil War. Longfellow's son, a lieutenant in the Union Army, had been seriously wounded, and while the poem reflected the father's sorrow and pain, it also showed his deep faith in God.

"Then pealed the bells more loud and deep:
God is not dead, nor doth He sleep.
With peace on earth, good will to men."

His inspiration for the poem came from the chiming of bells that Christmas Eve. The melody was written nine years later, and the song became a Christmas favorite.

Bells remain an important part of our Christmas ceremonies and observances today. Children fall asleep on Christmas Eve listening for the bells on Santa's sleigh and reindeer. Carolers carry bells; we use bells to decorate trees and other greenery; they appear on greeting cards. We tie bells on Christmas packages and love to hear the delightful tinkling sound they make when we shake the packages. We even bake cookies in bell shapes. Of course church bells ring out at midnight on Christmas Eve and on Christmas morning to call worshippers together. And we have all heard the bell ringers on the street corners who, each year, ask us to help celebrate the true meaning of Christmas by giving gifts of food or money to those who are less fortunate. This is another tradition with roots in medieval times when, during the Christmas season, the poor rang hand bells in the streets asking for alms.

The sound of bells ringing at Christmas is sweetly familiar to all of us, whether it is sleigh bells, jingle bells, or church bells. Christmas would certainly sound less cheerful without the sound of bells.

Remember what the angel Clarence said in *It's a Wonderful Life*? "Every time a bell rings, an angel gets his wings."

"Sleigh bells ring ... are you listening?..."

VI

On the First Day of Christmas, My True Love...

The Twelve Days Of Christmas

On the first day of Christmas,
My true love sent to me
  A partridge in a pear tree.

On the second day of Christmas,
  My true love sent to me
    Two turtledoves and
    A partridge in a pear tree.

On the third day of Christmas,
My true love sent to me
Three French hens,
Two turtledoves, and
  A partridge in a pear tree.

On the fourth day of Christmas,
My true love sent to me
Four colly birds,
Three French hens,
Two turtledoves, and
  A partridge in a pear tree.

On the fifth day of Christmas,
  My true love sent to me
Five gold rings,
Four colly birds,
Three French hens,
Two turtledoves, and
  A partridge in a pear tree.

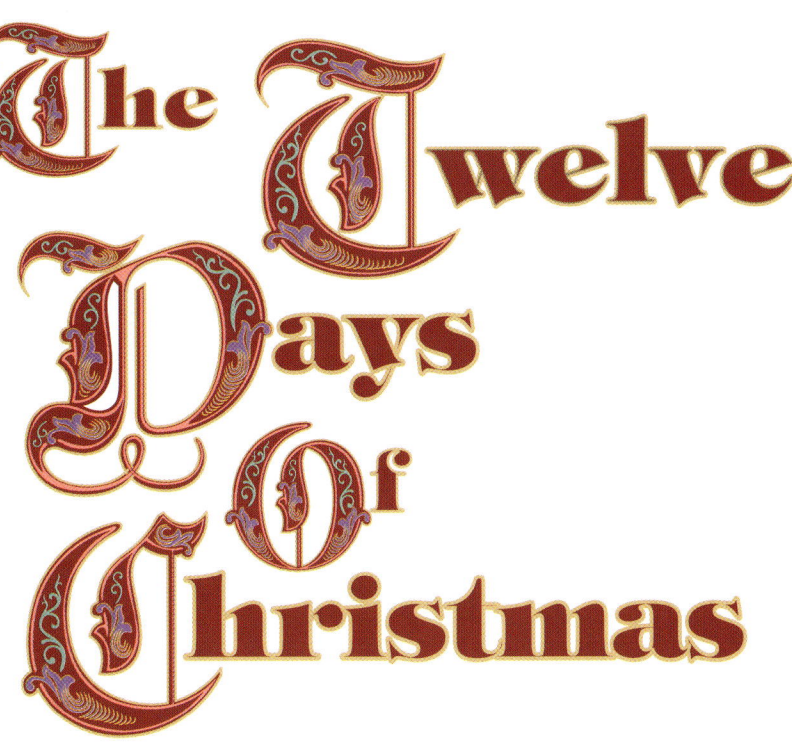

On the sixth day of Christmas,
My true love sent to me
Six geese a-laying,
Five gold rings,
Four colly birds,
Three French hens,
Two turtledoves, and
A partridge in a pear tree.

On the seventh day of Christmas,
My true love sent to me
Seven swans a-swimming,
Six geese a-laying,
Five gold rings,
Four colly birds,
Three French hens,
Two turtledoves, and
A partridge in a pear tree.

On the eighth day of Christmas,
My true love sent to me
Eight maids a-milking,
Seven swans a-swimming,
Six geese a-laying,
Five gold rings,
Four colly birds,
Three French hens,
Two turtledoves, and
A partridge in a pear tree.

On the ninth day of Christmas,
My true love sent to me
Nine drummers drumming,

Five gold rings,
Four colly birds,
Three French hens,

Eight maids a-milking,
Seven swans a-swimming,
Six geese a-laying,
Five gold rings,
    Four colly birds,
    Three French hens,
      Two turtledoves,
    and
        A partridge in
a pear tree.

Two turtledoves,
and
    A partridge in a pear tree.

    On the
tenth day of
Christmas,
My true love
sent to me
Ten pipers piping,
Nine drummers drumming,
Eight maids a-milking,
Seven swans a-swimming,
Six geese a-laying,

On the eleventh day of Christmas,
  My true love sent to me
  Eleven ladies dancing,
  Ten pipers piping,
  Nine drummers drumming,
  Eight maids a-milking,
  Seven swans a-swimming,
  Six geese a-laying,
  Five gold rings,
  Four colly birds,
  Three French hens,
  Two turtledoves, and
  A partridge in a pear tree.

On the twelfth day of Christmas,
  My true love sent to me
  Twelve fiddlers fiddling,
  Eleven ladies dancing,
  Ten pipers piping,
  Nine drummers drumming,
  Eight maids a-milking,
  Seven swans a-swimming,
  Six geese a-laying,
  Five gold rings,
  Four colly birds,
  Three French hens,
  Two turtledoves, and
  A partridge in a pear tree.

This version of *The Twelve Days of Christmas* was believed to be pagan in origin as counting songs often were. The first English version was printed in 1780 in a nursery book. In the Victorian era, the song became a popular parlor game of reciting the lines, with those who missed stanzas forfeiting something to the rest of the group. Today's version was published in England in 1842, and it is interesting to note the first seven presents are birds. The five gold rings allude to the five golden bands on the ring-necked pheasant and the four colly birds are blackbirds. *The Twelve Days of Christmas* was first heard in America in the 1940s and has become extremely popular since then.

An early French version of this song listed these gifts:
A good stuffing without bones,
Two breasts of veal,
Three joints of beef,
Four pigs' trotters,
Five legs of mutton,
Six partridges with cabbage,
Seven spitted rabbits,
Eight plates of salad,
Nine dishes from the chapter house,
Ten full casks,
Eleven beautiful maidens,
And twelve musketeers with swords.

Christmas: Traditions and Legends

On the First Day of Christmas

For God so loved the world that He gave His only begotten Son so that whosoever believeth in Him should not perish but have everlasting life."

God's gift to the world was His Son. The Wise Men brought gifts to His Son, and Christians around the world still exchange gifts in remembrance of His Son. Gift-giving at Christmas is an integral part of that celebration.

Christmas and gifts are synonymous — think of Santa and you think of presents; imagine a Christmas tree, and you think of presents piled under it; consider your friends and family, and you picture the gifts you will exchange.

Most of us can't imagine Christmas without the exchange of gifts. We remember cherished Christmas gifts we received as children, and delight in searching for special presents for our loved ones. We value the memories of anticipation on the faces of children sitting among a mound of wrapped treasures. We never really outgrow the thrill of seeing all the beautifully wrapped gifts under the tree, as we anticipate opening mysterious packages with our names on them. This holiday custom we enjoy so much began even before Christ was born.

Though the Wise Men brought the first Christmas gifts to the Christ Child, the tradition of exchanging gifts started long ago. Romans exchanged gifts called *strenae,* and this custom was part of their *Saturnalia* celebration. Subjects presented their rulers with green branches, usually laurel, olive or myrtle, symbolizing health, life and vigor. As the Roman empire spread north, the greens included ivy, rosemary, and holly, and simple branches were replaced with garlands and wreaths. Early Romans also exchanged "good luck" gifts of silver and gold to bring prosperity; sweets, such as honey, assuring the receiver sweetness in the coming year, and lamps symbolizing warmth and a year full of light.

When Christianity merged with pagan beliefs, gift-giving at Christmas time was another custom that was frowned upon by the church. For many years the church tried to prohibit gift-giving, but the people refused to give up this cherished tradition. Church leaders then sought to justify the practice by incorporating the concept that since Christ was a gift from God, giving gifts in His honor was appropriate.

Rulers of countries, who enjoyed the patronage of their subjects for many years, also insisted the custom continue. Caligula, a Roman ruler from 37 to 41 A. D. passed a law forcing his subjects to present him with gifts. Throughout the Middles Ages, English royalty demanded gifts from their subjects, as rulers had done in pagan times. Henry III, who ruled England from 1216-1272, was known to shut down merchants if they did not make ample cash contributions to him. It is rumored that Queen Elizabeth I collected most of her extensive wardrobe this way, including possibly the first pair of silk stockings seen in Europe. William the Conqueror reversed the custom and instead gave the Pope a large amount of money on December 25, 1067. However, the gift was not as generous as it appeared, since the money was seized by his army when it plundered Britain.

Though the practice of exchanging gifts at Christmas spread quickly throughout Europe, the date on which gifts were exchanged differed. In many countries gifts were exchanged on January 6, called the Twelfth Night, or Epiphany, the Greek word for manifestation, and was celebrated in Egypt and Greece before Christmas existed. This pagan festival honored rivers and water gods. When early eastern Christians began replacing the pagan celebration with a Christian one in the fourth century, they instituted the Feast of the Epiphany as a holy day commemorating Christ's baptism in the River Jordan.

In Sweden, gifts are exchanged on St. Lucia's Day, December 13. In Hungary, Holland and Poland, December 6 is a day for receiving presents since it is also St. Nicholas Day, named after the patron saint of children. Greek children do not receive gifts until January 1, St. Basil's Day, named after one of the four Fathers of the Greek Orthodox Church.

In England, December 26 is called "Boxing Day." Originally, the custom called for the village priest to open the "poor box" in church the day after Christmas and distribute the contents to the needy. Eventually, a custom evolved of giving "boxes" containing money to servants and tradespeople. The custom is similar to our present-day habit of tipping service people.

No one knows where the custom of wrapping presents started. In Denmark, gifts were wrapped so no one could possibly guess what was inside. Danes playfully used huge boxes for tiny gifts and any other disguise they could devise. Sometimes what was inside wasn't a gift at all, but a note telling the recipients where they could find the gift. Danes might wrap a present over and over, with a different name on each package, so the gift changed hands several times before it finally reached the right person. In Germany, gifts were given secretly, and finding out who they were from was considered bad luck. On Christmas Eve in the Netherlands, poems provided clues for a treasure hunt for gifts which were hidden by *Sinter Klaas*.

Wrapping presents is a nice custom, and it certainly makes Christmas morning more festive when you see all the pretty packages under the tree. But, anyone watching a four-year-old tear a package apart, completely ignoring its beautiful and carefully chosen wrappings and ribbon, might shake his head in bewilderment, wondering, "Why did I bother?"

The custom of gift-giving came from several sources. In times past, gifts were exchanged to honor the gods. The rich gave to the poor. Heads of countries demanded gifts from their subjects. The Wise Men brought gifts to the Baby Jesus, and St. Nicholas gave gifts to the children.

The gifts we give really aren't important. Why we give is. Giving gifts at Christmas is a tribute to the love we have for the Christ Child on His birthday, and to the the love we have for each other.

"And a partridge in a pear tree...."

Gift Of The Magi

O. Henry

One dollar and eighty-seven cents. That was all. And sixty cents of it was in pennies. Pennies saved one and two at a time by bulldozing the grocer and the vegetable man and the butcher until one's cheeks burned with the silent imputation of parsimony that such close dealing implied. Three times Della counted it. One dollar and eighty-seven cents. And the next day would be Christmas.

There was clearly nothing to do but flop down on the shabby little couch and howl. So Della did it. Which instigates the moral reflection that life is made up of sobs, sniffles and smiles, with sniffles predominating.

While the mistress of the home is gradually subsiding from the first stage to the second, take a look at the home. A furnished flat at eight dollars per week. It did not exactly beggar description, but it certainly had that word on the lookout for the mendicancy squad.

In the vestibule below was a letter-box into which no letter would go, and an electric button from which no mortal finger could coax a ring. Also appertaining thereunto was a card bearing the name "Mr. James Dillingham Young."

The "Dillingham" had been flung to the breeze during a former period of prosperity when its possessor was being paid $30 per week. Now, when the income was shrunk to $20, the letters of "Dillingham" looked blurred, as though they were thinking seriously of contracting to a modest and unassuming D. But whenever Mr. James Dillingham Young came home and reached his flat above he was called "Jim" and greatly hugged by Mrs. James Dillingham Young, already introduced to you as Della. Which is all very good.

Della finished her cry and attended to her cheeks with the powder rag. She stood by the window and looked out dully at a gray cat walking a gray fence in a gray backyard. Tomorrow would be Christmas Day, and she had only $1.87 with which to buy Jim a present. She had been saving every penny she could for months, with this result. Twenty dollars a week doesn't go far. Expenses had been greater than she had calculated. They always are. Only $1.87 to buy a present for Jim. Her Jim. Many a happy hour she had been planning for something nice for him. Something fine and rare and sterling — something just a little bit near to being worthy of the honor of being owned by Jim.

There was a pier-glass between the windows

of the room. Perhaps you have seen a pier-glass in an $8 flat. A very thin and very agile person may, by observing his reflection in a rapid sequence of longitudinal strips, obtain a fairly accurate conception of his looks. Della, being slender, had mastered the art.

Suddenly she whirled from the window and stood before the glass. Her eyes were shining brightly, but her face had lost its color within twenty seconds. Rapidly she pulled down her hair and let it fall to its full length.

Now, there were two possessions of the James Dillingham Young's in which they both took a mighty pride. One was Jim's gold watch that had been his father's and his grandfather's. The other was Della's hair. Had the Queen of Sheba lived in the flat across the airshaft, Della would have let her hair hang out the window some day to dry just to depreciate Her Majesty's jewels and gifts. Had King Solomon been the janitor, with all his treasures piled up in the basement, Jim would have pulled out his watch every time he passed, just to see him pluck at his beard from envy.

So now Della's beautiful hair fell about her rippling and shining like a cascade of brown waters. It reached below her knee and made itself almost a garment for her. And then she did it up again nervously and quickly. Once she faltered for a minute and stood still while a tear or two splashed on the worn red carpet.

On went her old brown jacket; on went her old brown hat. With a whirl of skirts and with the brilliant sparkle still in her eyes, she fluttered out the door and down the stairs into the street.

Where she stopped the sign read: "Mme Sofronie. Hair Goods of All Kinds." One flight up Della ran, and collected herself, panting. Madame, large, too white, chilly, hardly looked the "Sofronie."

"Will you buy my hair?" asked Della.

"I buy hair," said Madame. "Take yer hat off and let's have a sight at the looks of it."

Down rippled the brown cascade.

"Twenty dollars," said Madame, lifting the mass with a practiced hand.

"Give it to me quick," said Della.

Oh, and the next two hours tripped by on rosy wings. Forget the hashed metaphor. She was ransacking the stores for Jim's present.

She found it at last. It surely had been made for Jim and no one else. There was no other like it in any of the stores, and she had turned all of them inside out. It was a platinum fob chain simple and chaste in design, properly proclaiming its value by substance alone and not by meretricious ornamentation — as all good things should do. It was even worthy of The Watch. As soon as she saw it she knew it must be Jim's. It was like him. Quietness and value — the description applied to both. Twenty-one dollars they took from her for it, and she hurried home with the 87 cents. With that chain on his watch Jim might be properly anxious about the time in any company. Grand as the watch was, he sometimes looked at it on the sly on account of the old leather strap that he used in place of a chain.

When Della reached home, her intoxication gave way a little to prudence and reason. She got out her curling irons and lighted the gas and went to work repairing the ravages made by generosity added to love. Which is always a tremendous task, dear friends — a mammoth task.

Within forty minutes her head was covered with tiny, close-lying curls that made her look wonderfully like a truant schoolboy. She looked at her reflection in the mirror long, carefully, and critically.

"If Jim doesn't kill me," she said to herself, "before he takes a second look at me, he'll say I look like a Coney Island chorus girl. But what could I do — oh! What could I do with a dollar and eighty-seven cents?"

At seven o'clock, the coffee was made and the frying pan was on the back of the stove hot and ready to cook the chops.

Jim was never late. Della doubled the fob chain in her hand and sat on the corner of the table near the door that he always entered. Then she heard his step on the stairway down on the first flight, and she turned white for just a minute. She had a habit of saying little silent prayers about the simplest everyday things, and now she whispered: "Please God, make him think I am still pretty."

The door opened and Jim stepped in and closed it. He looked thin and very serious. Poor fellow, he was only twenty-two and to be burdened with a family! He needed a new overcoat and he was without gloves.

Jim stepped inside the door, as immovable as a setter at the scent of quail. His eyes were fixed upon Della, and there was an expression in them that she could not read, and it terrified her. It was not anger, nor surprise, nor disapproval, nor horror, nor any of the sentiments that she had been prepared for. He simply stared at her fixedly with that peculiar expression on his face.

Della wriggled off the table and went for him.

"Jim, darling," she cried, "don't look at me that way. I had my hair cut off and sold it because I couldn't have lived through Christmas without giving you a present. It'll grow out again — you won't mind, will you? I just had to do it. My hair grows awfully fast. Say 'Merry Christmas!' Jim, and let's be happy. You don't know what a nice — what a beautiful, nice gift I've got for you."

"You've cut off your hair?" asked Jim, laboriously, as if he had not arrived at that patent fact yet even after the hardest mental labor.

"Cut it off and sold it," said Della. "Don't you like me just as well, anyhow? I'm me without my hair, ain't I?"

Jim looked about the room curiously.

"You say your hair is gone?" he said, with an air almost of idiocy.

"You needn't look for it," said Della. "It's sold, I tell you — sold and gone, too. It's Christmas Eve, boy. Be good to me, for it went for you. Maybe the hairs on my head were numbered," she went on with a sudden serious sweetness, "but nobody could ever count my love for you. Shall I put the chops on, Jim?"

Out of his trance Jim seemed quickly to wake. He enfolded his Della. For ten seconds let us regard with tense scrutiny some inconsequential object in the other direction. Eight dollars a week or a million a year — what is the difference? A mathematician or a wit would give you the wrong answer. The Magi brought valuable gifts, but that was not among them. This dark assertion will be illuminated later on.

Jim drew a package from his overcoat pocket and threw it upon the table.

"Don't make any mistake, Della," he said, "about me. I don't think there's anything in the way of a haircut or a shave or a shampoo that could make me like my girl any less. But if you'll unwrap that package you may see why you had me going for a while at first."

White fingers and nimble tore at the string and paper. And then an ecstatic scream of joy; and then, alas! a quick feminine change to hysterical tears and wails, necessitating the immediate employment of all the comforting powers of the lord of the flat.

For there lay The Combs — the set of combs, side and back, that Della had worshiped for long in a Broadway window. Beautiful combs, pure tortoise shell, with jewelled rims — just the shade to wear in the beautiful vanished hair. They were expensive combs, she knew, and her heart had simply craved and yearned over them without the least hope of possession. And now, they were hers, but the tresses that should have adorned the coveted adornments were gone.

But she hugged them to her bosom, and at length she was able to look up with dim eyes and a smile and say: "My hair grows so fast, Jim!"

And then Della leaped up like a little singed cat and cried, "Oh, oh!"

Jim had not yet seen his beautiful present. She held it out to him eagerly upon her open palm. The dull precious metal seemed to flash with a reflection of her bright and ardent spirit.

"Isn't it a dandy, Jim? I hunted all over town to find it. You'll have to look at the time a hundred times a day now. Give me your watch. I want to see how it looks on it."

Instead of obeying, Jim tumbled on the couch and put his hands under the back of his head and smiled.

"Dell," said he, "let's put our Christmas presents away and keep 'em a while. They're too nice to use just as a present. I sold the watch to get the money to buy your combs. And now suppose you put the chops on."

The Magi, as you know, were wise men — wonderfully wise men — who brought gifts to the Babe in the manger. They invented the art of giving Christmas presents. Being wise, their gifts were no doubt wise ones, possibly bearing the privilege of exchange in case of duplication. And here I have lamely related to you the uneventful chronicle of two foolish children in a flat who most unwisely sacrificed for each other the greatest treasures of their house. But in a last word to the wise of these days let it be said that of all who give and receive gifts, such as they are wisest. Everywhere they are wisest. They are the Magi.

VII

Hark! The Herald Angels Sing

Hark! The Herald Angels Sing

Can you imagine Christmas without music? It is just not possible to conceive of this joyous holiday without the wonderful, familiar music that goes with it. As Christmas approaches and we hear the well-known songs, it is like welcoming home an old friend, and is often the first sign that the holiday season is on its way. Wherever Christ's birth is celebrated, He is honored in song. The Bible reveals that the very first Christmas carol was sung by angels on that first Christmas Eve: "Glory to God in the highest, and on earth, peace and good will toward men." Perhaps the angels were accompanied by shepherds' flutes and animals bleating.

St. Francis of Assisi is often credited with popularizing Christmas carols. In 1224, in Greccio, Italy, when he re-created the nativity scene on Christmas Eve, he invited the children in attendance to join him in singing carols to honor the Baby Jesus. As the custom grew, this scene was repeated throughout Europe, and adults joined children in singing carols.

Singing has always been part of the celebration at festivals; pagans sang songs of praise, joy and glory in honor of their gods and goddesses. When Christianity began, those songs that were part of the pagan tradition were adopted by Christians who changed the words to praise their God. As Christianity spread from country to country, so did the music.

The word "carol" originally referred to songs associated with round dances or ring dances. Ring dances began with the Greeks and Romans, who formed a circle, joined hands, and walked around, much like the game, "Ring Around the Rosey." Dancers were often accompanied by flute music, which was later replaced by singing. Dancers then moved to the rhythm of the singing voices, and carols came to mean singing instead of dancing. Our merry-go-round, or carousel, is from the word "carole."

At times of merrymaking, carols were popular songs with simple feelings, easy to sing and to remember the lyrics. They often had a refrain which was repeated, such as: "Fa la la la la la la la la." Some carols were originally lullabies or folksongs passed from generation to generation by word of mouth. These "folk songs" came from small villages, and it is believed priests preserved them by recording them in writing.

Because some of the original carols once had been folksongs, ballads or lullabies, they were not considered devout enough to be played or heard in churches. Because these melodies were happy and gay, they were even considered irreverent by some. In fact, the custom of caroling, or singing in the streets, started with these light melodies. Strolling musicians called troubadours, played in the streets of villages or in front of homes, a custom that is still enjoyed in many countries. Often, professional singers, or waits, accompanied them, and together they "walked the parish" with music at Christmastime. Hand bell ringers sometimes joined in. A candle in the window of a home meant that carolers were welcome and usually a treat or money awaited them. Caroling is deeply rooted in British tradition, tracing its origin to medieval times when groups visited castles and sang for their supper.

As Christmas became more popular around the world, carols that told the story of the birth of Christ were accepted as part of the religious observance. Though their origin is difficult to trace, hymns generally were written by known composers and consisted of more elaborate scores and phrasing. One appreciable difference between hymns and carols is that hymns are more somber and are sung in honor or praise of God, while carols may be religious but may just tell a tale of a red-nosed reindeer.

It is interesting to trace how our familiar hymns came to be. *Nowel* or *nouel*, a French word meaning Christmas or carol, is probably derived from the Latin word *natalis* or *natal,* which means birth. It became *nowell*, then *noel,* in English, meaning "Now all is well." This is the message of angels to the shepherds in our well-loved hymn, *The First Noel.* This lovely song proclaims the birth of Christ and is one of the oldest carols.

"Noel, Noel, born is the King of Israel."

One of our favorite and familiar carols, *O Little Town of Bethlehem,* was written in 1868 by Bishop Phillips Brooks of Massachusetts.

Dr. Brooks visited Bethlehem, riding horseback through the fields from Jerusalem to Bethlehem on Christmas Eve. He was moved by the sight of the shepherds in the fields, and the "little town of Bethlehem" shining in the starlight much as he imagined it was on the night Christ was born. This image of that extraordinary evening lingered in his mind long after he returned home.

Dr. Brooks was especially fond of hearing children sing in his church, so three years later he wrote the words for a song they could perform in the annual Sunday School Christmas program. He asked his choir director, Lewis H. Redner, to write the music. Although Redner tried, he was unable to create a simple melody to accompany Dr. Brooks' words. Finally, the night before the children were to perform, Redner awakened at midnight and the melody, which he described as "a gift from heaven," came to him. They hastily printed the words and music on leaflets, and on Christmas morning, thirty-six children sang,

*"O, little town of Bethlehem,
How still we see thee lie…"*

Servicemen who were stationed far from their loved ones during the holidays recount how the music of Christmas brought them closer to home. Group-singing of familiar carols made them less lonely and homesick even in the middle of a thick jungle or in a lonely trench in a strange land. "You wouldn't think of gathering together and singing songs any time other than Christmas," one explained.

There is a story told of French and German soldiers during the Franco-Prussian War in 1870. It was Christmas Eve outside of Paris, which was under siege. Troops from both sides were in trenches facing each other. Suddenly, a young Frenchman jumped out of his trench, stood up, and sang, in a chillingly beautiful, but also very loud voice, *O Holy Night*. The Germans were so awestruck that no one fired a shot. As soon as the last powerful notes faded, a German soldier stood in his trench and responded with an equally lovely German Christmas hymn. After a similar event during World War I in France, the soldiers on opposing sides exchanged chocolates and other small gifts, and the guns of war were temporarily silenced. In 1914, in what has been called the Christmas Truce of the First World War, Germans and Saxons of the North Staffordshire Regiment, exchanged greetings, then held a songfest suggested by one of the British soldiers. German and British soldiers took turns performing their beloved and familiar Christmas songs, and a truce was declared until midnight Christmas Day. While the truce was in effect, the troops helped each other bury their dead. At midnight, after both sides fired warning shots into the air, the killing resumed.

Some Christmas songs don't even mention the birth of Christ but contain other reminders of the holiday season. *Jingle Bells, It's Beginning to Look a Lot Like Christmas, Winter Wonderland, Santa Claus is Coming to Town, Frosty the Snowman*, and, of course, *Rudolph the Red-Nosed Reindeer* (® Robert L. May Co., Novato, California) are happy songs we associate with Christmas just like the hymns and carols written in early centuries. Lyrics like "chestnuts roasting on an open fire" are as familiar as "from angels bending near the earth," and may be even more familiar to those of us who love all the songs of Christmas.

One of the most popular American Christmas songs was written in 1942 for a movie. Irving Berlin wrote *White Christmas* while America was at war, and it soon became a symbol of homesick servicemen dreaming about returning home to their families, "I'm dreaming of a white Christmas, just like the ones I used to know…" After the popularity of *White Christmas*, snow became almost essential at Christmas, even if it had to be artificial snow in places like Miami and Maui.

Today we sing familiar Christmas songs in town squares, shopping malls, schools and churches. We cherish the opportunity to join in with family and friends at parties and festive gatherings. Like soldiers far from home, this may be the only time of year we join together and remember the songs we learned as children.

Christmas would indeed be less joyous without the songs of the season. Attending a church service Christmas Eve and joining a full choir while a darkened church glows with candlelight is an experience that brings a rare sense of belonging. It is the beautiful, beloved music at Christmas that helps us all spread the message of love and peace.

Silent Night

It was Christmas Eve in 1818, in the little village of Oberndorf, Austria, where Father Josef Mohr was the assistant pastor in the local parish. Father Mohr was extremely upset that the church organ was inoperable because mice had gnawed away at the bellows. "We must have something special for Christmas Eve Midnight Mass," he told the organist, Franz Gruber. "Without music, it will not seem like Christmas at all."

Oberndorf was a small village, and the parishioners did not have the time or the tools to fix the organ. The organist paced the floor, trying to think of a solution. It was getting late, but Father Mohr still had to make some calls in his parish. He had been summoned to the cottage of a woodcutter and his wife to welcome and bless their newborn baby. When he entered the woodcutter's cottage, Father Mohr gasped at the sight before him. The mother cradled her newborn baby in her arms; the father stood by adoringly. Father Mohr felt as though he was reliving the night in Bethlehem so many years ago.

When he started toward home, it was late and very dark. Father Mohr stopped on a hill overlooking the snow-covered village. The lights of the homes below sparkled in the deep wintry night. All around him was still and quiet.

As he stood there in the majestic stillness of that wintry night, Father Mohr thought, "It must have been a night like this — that silent and holy night in Bethlehem."

Father Mohr hurried back to his office in the church, sat down and wrote his thoughts in poetic form. All his fatigue and weariness disappeared as the words flowed from his pen. When he finished, he sent for the organist, Franz Gruber, who burst into his room and threw up his hands in despair, because he had failed to find a solution to the organ problem.

"Forget about the decrepit old pipe organ," Father Mohr told him. "Write some music to this poem, and we will sing it at Mass, organ or no organ." He then handed the organist a guitar.

"I am an organist, I am not a guitarist," he loudly protested, but Father Mohr refused to listen.

"Surely you can play three chords on the guitar," he said. "Write your music on three chords and keep it simple. You play the music on the guitar, and you and I will sing this new carol at the service. Surely the congregation will not miss the organ if they are hearing their priest and organist singing together for the first time."

He was right. The people were so moved by the beautiful carol they did not miss the organ at all. Perhaps they knew a special gift had been given the Christ Child on His birthday: a beautiful song to honor Him. *Silent Night* became one of the most beloved of all Christmas carols … "Christ the Saviour is born, Christ the Saviour is born."

"And heaven and nature sing.…"

Christmas: Traditions and Legends

Do You Hear What I Hear?

After the Sunday school class sang Silent Night and heard the Christmas story, the teacher suggested her pupils draw the nativity scene. A little boy finished first. The teacher praised his drawing of the manger, of Joseph, Mary and the Infant. But she was puzzled by a roly-poly figure off to one side and asked who it was. "Oh," explained the youngster, "that's Round John Virgin."

– Reader's Digest, December 1958

VIII

Deck the Halls

Deck The Halls

The custom of decorating homes on festive occasions has been practiced worldwide for thousands of years. This practice is neither pagan nor Christian. In times past, pagans living in Germany worshiped trees since Germany was a country covered with forests. They brought evergreen branches inside to provide shelter for the wood sprites they believed lived in the trees. Other Europeans cut cherry tree branches and brought them indoors, hoping they would bloom at Christmas time, and bring good luck in the coming year. Some cultures worshiped evergreens which represented eternal life, and they held festivals in the deepest winter to insure the return of the sun. The sun was essential to their existence, and they believed the evergreens held magic power by virtue of their perennial greenness when all other plants lost their leaves in winter and became withered and dormant.

The Romans decorated their homes, temples, and statues of their gods with green branches, garlands, and plants, using fir, pine and spruce branches, as well as holly, ivy and mistletoe. People wore green laurel wreaths on their heads and carried small trees lighted with candles. Some believed the spirits of the woods wandered restlessly in the cold during winter solstice, and welcoming them indoors into the warmth would bring good luck during the coming year.

To entice these woodland creatures inside, people hung greenery on their doors and in their windows, especially holly, which was a symbol of joy and peace. They also believed greenery protected them against the evils of darkness and from ghosts who might want to steal indoors to get warm. Thus, evergreens held the promise of a new year, new crops and assurance the sun would return, and ultimately were a symbol of survival. The Christian Church gradually accepted this custom as harmless and eventually not only adopted it but expanded on it in homes and churches.

Holly was one of the best-loved greens. With its bright red berries and shiny green leaves, it proved the sun never deserted the earth even during the darkest, bleakest months. It was a custom to plant a holly bush near the home so it would protect the inhabitants from lightning, thunder and other severe weather. Holly wreaths were hung in homes to ward off witches, who supposedly feared holly, and it was even placed on bedposts to assure pleasant dreams. Many believed Christ's crown of thorns was made of holly, and that the berries were white before the crucifixion, but turned red with His blood. Another legend says the robin got his red breast from plucking thorns from Christ's crown at Calvary. It is thought that the red and green colors associated with Christmas originated with holly.

In English carols, the holly is considered male and the ivy is female. Legends describe how the holly, with its prickly leaves and red berries represents the male reproductive urge. It was also claimed to be a "man's plant" because it protects itself with thorns as a man would protect himself with weapons. The ivy was known as the "woman's plant" because it entwined and embraced whatever was near, or because it needed the support of a wall or tree, as, according to old beliefs, women needed the support of men.

One story about these plants recounts an episode when an English knight who was hosting a party, asked for the attention of the guests after all were seated. He said to the men (the holly), "Before you eat, whoever among you is master of your wife shall now stand and so declare." Several minutes passed with none of the men moving. Finally, down at the far end of the table, a man stood up and spoke — albeit very briefly and softly.

Then the knight turned to the ladies (the ivy): "Now it is your turn. Whoever among you is master of your husband, let her stand and speak as proof." Whereupon all the ladies rose in unison and spoke very loudly, again in unison. "Ah." exclaimed the knight. "There can be no doubt: the ivy is the master."

Another legend tells us why we use holly in decorating at Christmas. On the first Christmas night, when the shepherds left their flocks and hurried to the manger to find the Baby Jesus, a tiny lamb followed a shepherd boy who was caring for him. The baby lamb was quite weak because he had been ill, but was afraid to stay alone in the fields, so he struggled to keep up. No one heard his faint bleating sounds, or someone might have picked him up and carried him. It was hard to see in the dark, and the lamb stumbled on a rock and fell, scratching himself on a prickly holly bush. The thorns cut into him and, according to the legend, the red berries on the holly are the lamb's blood that froze into drops on the branches.

There were many stories about trees and flowers blooming out of season the night Christ was born, especially the Glastonbury thorn and the Christmas rose. Many of the early Christians hung greenery over their doors to show that the spirit of Christ lived inside, thus transforming old superstitions into new meanings.

The round shape of wreaths most likely originated with early Christians who hung up wagon wheels decorated with evergreens and lighted candles. Since the ancient Greeks and Romans wore laurel wreaths as a symbol of victory and glory, it's been suggested this custom could also be the origin of the Christmas wreaths. However, many Christians believe Christ's crown of thorns was the true origin of the shape of Christmas wreaths. Over time, wreaths on doors at Christmas came to signify peace and a welcome to all.

The poinsettia has become known as the Christmas flower. A native plant of Mexico and South America, it grows best in tropical and subtropical regions, where it reaches heights of up to fifteen feet. In cold climates, the brilliant red plant must be grown indoors. The poinsettia was first introduced to America in 1836 by Dr. Joel R. Poinsett, the first United States ambassador to Mexico. Today, it is the most popular of all Christmas flowers or plants. In fact, more poinsettias are sold in America than any other potted plant. Actually, it is not a flower, it is a plant with green and red leaves and a yellow center, which is the blossom. According to Christmas legend, the center represents the Star of Bethlehem.

Another Christmas tradition is the bayberry, which we usually associate with scented candles. There is an old legend that the bay tree gave shelter to the Holy Family during a storm, and since that day lightning will never strike the tree. There is another old belief that sweethearts separated during the holidays will be united the following year if each lights a bayberry candle.

The popular Christmas cactus that blooms in the winter is a native of Brazil, where it grows on the branches and trunks of trees, much like mistletoe. The cactus roots into moss and derives moisture from rain.

Today, rosemary is a popular herb used to season food. However, in the Middle Ages, it was strewn on floors of homes to sweeten the room. Rosemary was loved for its fragrance as well as its beautiful lavender color. According to another Christmas legend, the lavender color came from Mary's cloak when she tossed it over a rosemary bush during the Holy Family's flight to Egypt. The legend tells us that the rosemary's sweet scent comes from the Baby Jesus' blanket, which Mary spread over the herb during their journey.

As we've seen, greenery was originally brought indoors to bring cheer to the pagans in the dark of winter. It has remained a significant part of our holiday decorating in town malls and squares, yards of churches and homes, and city streets all over the world. When the world outside our window reveals the bleak palette of mid-winter, the brilliance of evergreen trees and plants brighten even the gloomiest day, bringing cheer to everyone during the Christmas season, as in ancient times.

"Tis the season to be jolly....."

Doris Baines

Mistletoe

In the mystical language of flowers, mistletoe means, "Give me a kiss." In Celtic languages, it was called "all heal."

There are many legends about the mistletoe. One suggests how mistletoe got its name: Someone spotted a bird, called the "missel thrush," with a white berry stuck to its toe and formed the word "misseltoe," which became mistletoe. One belief associated with mistletoe warned that if a girl was not kissed under the plant during Christmas, she would not marry in the coming year.

Mistletoe is actually a semi-parasite which grows on the top branches of host trees, usually the oak. In ancient times, it was believed to be sacred, to have come from heaven, possessing mystic powers because it grew without roots and never touched the ground. During the winter solstice, the ancient Druids wore white robes and climbed oak trees to cut down mistletoe with a sickle. They caught it in a white cloth, since it was believed if the mistletoe touched the ground, witches would steal it and cause it to lose its magical power.

Mistletoe was also regarded as a symbol of the sun, a giver of life and protector against disease and poison. Druids offered cut branches in prayer to their gods, as a token of peace and prosperity. The plant was believed to encourage romance, to bring happiness and good luck, and to promote peace.

Despite all these positive beliefs, mistletoe was the only plant banned from churches, since it was the one most identified with pagan superstitions. The English Church banned its use by Christians until sometime around 1600. Some Christians believed mistletoe was originally a tree whose wood was used to make the cross on which Christ was crucified, and that it shrank from shame into a parasite bush.

Even today, mistletoe is rarely seen in church decorations. A notable exception to this rule occurred during the Middle Ages in the Cathedral of York. Each Christmas Eve, a priest ceremoniously placed a large sprig of mistletoe on the altar of the church. The mistletoe remained there for twelve days, during which time prisoners were released, beggars were given food and shelter, and a joyous Yuletide festivity was celebrated. The plant was used as a symbol of Christ, the Divine Healer.

In the late eighteenth century, people in England began using the mistletoe in their home Christmas decorations. They forgot the pagan customs associated with mistletoe, and kept the beliefs that the plant brought happiness, peace and luck. They created the "kissing ball," or "kissing bunch" which held the mistletoe inside and was hung where guests would walk under it. It provided a wonderful opportunity and did not require a reason for kissing.

The Legend Of Mistletoe

(why we kiss under the mistletoe)

Baldur was a Norse god of light and spring, purity and beauty. He was the beloved son of Frigga, the Norse goddess of love and marriage. Baldur was disturbed by dreams that his life was in danger. When he told his mother about his fears, she traveled throughout the land, demanding promises from all the other gods and all the natural elements — fire, water, air and earth — not to harm her son. But, in her desperate haste to protect Baldur, Frigga forgot to speak to the mistletoe, which she considered too puny and insignificant to do him harm.

Baldur had one enemy, Loki, another god known for causing mischief and evil toward his fellow gods. Loki was very jealous of Baldur and, upon learning that Frigga had ignored the mistletoe, Loki convinced the blind god, Holder, to hurl a mistletoe dart into Baldur's heart, killing him.

Frigga was heartbroken when she learned of Baldur's death and wept many, many tears. Her bitter tears fell onto the mistletoe, clustered on the sprigs, and turned into pearl-like berries.

Frigga was a good and powerful goddess, and she pleaded with the other gods to bring Baldur back to life. They all loved Baldur and, hearing of Loki's terrible vengeance, they agreed. Frigga was delighted and stood under the mistletoe's white berries, kissing everyone who passed under them. She then declared that the mistletoe would never again be used as a weapon and said, "All who stand beneath the mistletoe must kiss in friendship and peace."

It is said the myth of the mistletoe spread throughout the land, and whenever enemies met under it, they laid down their weapons and declared a truce.

"All who stand beneath the mistletoe must kiss in friendship and peace.…"

The Glastonbury Thorn Legend

Joseph of Arimathea was a member of the senate in Palestine. He was a kind man who became a Christian before Christ was crucified. Being a devout follower of Jesus made his life difficult because Christianity was unpopular in those days. Those who declared their Christian affiliation had many enemies, but Joseph was not deterred. He knew Christ would be with him in whatever he did.

According to the gospel of Saint Luke, after Christ was crucified, it was Joseph who approached Pilate and asked that he be given His body to bury.

"And taking it down, he wrapped it in linen, and placed it in a rock-hewn tomb, in which none had yet been buried."

Joseph did this gladly, as he believed it essential that Christ be laid to rest after He was crucified. Unfortunately, this unselfish act made his life even harder.

Joseph had traveled to England many times as a merchant, and in 70 A.D. after Jesus died he decided to move there to preach Christianity. He was not a young man when he made this decision, but Joseph knew it was the right choice.

The journey by boat took many weeks, and Joseph and his traveling companions were weary. It was Christmas Eve, and they had stopped to rest on the English coast near the town of Glastonbury. Joseph left the boat to climb alone to the top of Wearyall Hill, overlooking the harbor. Because of his age, Joseph walked with a staff made of hawthorn wood. As he stood on top of the hill waiting for his friends to join him, he thrust the staff into the ground to support his weary body.

The soil in Glastonbury was soft and spongy, and the instant the staff pierced the earth, it took root. Branches sprouted, and green leaves and buds miraculously appeared on the branches. Joseph's companions from the boat were approaching him as this happened, and as they all watched in amazement, the buds opened into fragrant blossoms.

Joseph's companions stopped in disbelief, but Joseph knew this was a miracle, a sign from God that his journey had ended. He would stay in Glastonbury and spread the gospel of Christianity.

The staff grew into a healthy and beautiful tree. It bloomed each Christmas Eve, even in snow and the coldest winter when all other trees were barren. Its sweet-scented blossoms became a symbol of miraculous healing. For centuries, people who were ill journeyed to Glastonbury to touch the branches, believing they may have healing powers.

During the time of the Puritans' influence in England, these beliefs were declared superstitious and sacrilegious, and a member of the church decided to chop down Joseph's tree. After growing for many years, the tree had two trunks. Legend claims that the Puritan cut the first trunk easily, but when he tried to chop down the second, a chip flew up, striking him in the eye and blinding him.

Though the tree had been split, it continued to grow and bloom each Christmas Eve, and cuttings from it were planted around the world. The original tree continues to bloom in Glastonbury, in the same spot where centuries ago, Joseph of Arimathea planted it.

The Legend Of Poinsettias

In Mexico, it is an old custom to take flowers to church on Christmas Eve and place them at the altar in honor of the Christ Child.

Mario was nine years old and lived in a small village in the mountains of Mexico. Each Christmas Eve, as far back as he could remember, Mario watched the villagers, their arms filled with beautiful flowers, walk past his modest home on their way to the church. Mario had always wished he could join them and bring a flower or a plant to show how much he, too, loved the Baby Jesus.

Mario was too poor to buy flowers, but each year he spent the days before Christmas walking through the fields searching for wildflowers that might have survived the cold, bitter winter. Each year he would return home empty-handed, disappointed and sad. Still, one year when the villagers passed by his house on their way to the church, Mario could not resist following them.

As they neared the church, Mario fell further and further behind and began to cry. He watched all the people enter the church, carrying their lovely bouquets and plants, and fell to his knees, sobbing. "I, too, want to bring a beautiful flower to the Christ Child, but I am too poor to buy anything, and I could not find a flower. I would love to go into the church, but I cannot."

As he knelt on the ground, the little boy heard a rustling sound behind him.

"Mario," a voice said. Mario froze with fear. "Mario," the voice repeated, "look back here behind those tall weeds."

It was a sweet, gentle voice, and somehow Mario knew he didn't need to be afraid. Mario looked up but saw no one. He brushed aside the weeds, which he had not noticed earlier. There, before him, stood a stone angel. A soft glow of light seemed to surround her.

"Mario," she instructed, "pick up the weeds that are growing where you kneel and take them into the church for the Christ Child."

Mario stared up through his tears and cried, "But I cannot take weeds to the Baby Jesus."

"Mario," the angel gently replied, "the simplest gift, when given with love, will be the most beautiful to Him."

Mario began to pull weeds as fast as he

could, as he knew the church service was about to begin. He was so busy gathering the weeds, he did not even notice that the angel had disappeared. Mario was also certain everyone would notice he was carrying a pitiful handful of weeds to the Christ Child and would laugh at him. And he was certainly not convinced the Christ Child would think they were beautiful, but he did not have time to worry. Instead, he gathered the weeds in his arms and hurried up the steps of the church.

When Mario entered the church, his heart was pounding so hard, he was certain everyone could hear it. But he had stopped crying, and he stood straight and tall as he marched down the aisle toward the altar. Starlight beamed through the stained-glass windows, and a cloak of brilliant colors fell on him as he strode along. Mario was overwhelmed at the sight of all the candles glowing at the altar.

"I know this is the most beautiful sight in the whole world," Mario thought. He completely forgot he was carrying a humble gift of weeds as he walked on bravely. Suddenly, the Baby Jesus' crib was in front of him.

Mario carefully placed the weeds near the Christ Child's crib, then, kneeling, he buried his head and whispered, "These are for you, dear Christ Child, and they are given with all my love. I am only sorry I do not have lovely…"

Mario did not finish his sentence because, as he spoke, he looked up to see the most astonishing thing — the brown stalks of the weeds were turning green, and the withered dead leaves were turning into a beautiful scarlet-red flower.

Mario could not believe his eyes. It was the prettiest flower he had ever seen. Tears streamed down his cheeks, but this time they were tears of pride and joy. Mario was so overwhelmed he did not notice that all the villagers, who had also witnessed this miracle, now knelt in the church.

Mario understood what the angel had told him. He knew that the most important gift for the Christ Child was the one he gave gladly — the gift of love.

IX

O' Christmas Tree, O' Christmas Tree

O Christmas Tree, O Christmas Tree

We've all heard these comments and more. Yet, each year the family, especially the youngsters, excitedly anticipates the adventure of choosing the tree which will take its place in our holiday celebration. The selection process itself is an exhausting undertaking. Each family member is searching for the perfect tree, and the children compete for this honor with determination unlike anything you have witnessed since last year's trek.

"I found the best one," comes from a row somewhere within shouting distance.

"Stay right there," you reply.

"I've got a perfect one, better than we've ever had," from the opposite direction.

"Stay with it, I'll be right there," you answer.

This can go on for hours as you post your children by the chosen trees, only to find they have found a better one, which they want to compare to the first one, only they can't remember where the first one was.

When you finally resolve the situation and take the tree home, some of the family members will be happy and some may pout. However, once inside the house where the excitement of decorating takes over, all else is forgotten and the season becomes official. You've got your tree — now Christmas is really here.

When we stop to consider, it truly is an odd custom — bringing a once-living tree into our home for three or four weeks, sticking it in water so it will stay "fresh," rearranging furniture so it will fit, and then hanging as many decorations as possible on every branch from top to bottom.

It is usually a family affair, from tree selection to setting the star or angel on the tree top. Fond memories unfold as we unpack our treasured decorations collected over the years, and recall where they came from or who made them. This beloved custom began centuries ago, and over

> *"It's too tall..."*
> *"It's too skinny..."*
> *"It's too full..."*
> *"It's crooked..."*
> *"It's got a big hole in it..."*
> *"It's brown on one side..."*
> *"It's flat on one side..."*

Christmas: Traditions and Legends

the years was observed by people in many countries.

In some ancient cultures, trees were worshiped as a symbol of life. Egyptians brought date palms indoors to celebrate the winter solstice. Druids decorated trees with lighted candles to honor their gods Odin and Baldur, and tied apples to the branches as thanks to the gods for giving them fruit. Romans hung masks of Bacchus — their god of wine and revelry — on tree branches believing they would bear more fruit. In the tenth century, Christians first started bringing fruit or blossoming trees indoors in the winter to force blooming, believing they would bring good luck. With Christianity established, the tree became a symbol of Jesus as the Tree of Life.

The earliest historical reference to a "Christmas" tree was in the sixteenth century in Latvia and Estonia. In 1510 and 1514, two Christmas tree celebrations were noted. At each ceremony, after a festive dinner on Christmas Eve, two village merchants took the tree, decorated with artificial roses, to the town square where villagers danced around it, then set fire to it.

Another account from an anonymous visitor to Strasbourg in 1605, describes small fir trees set up in the parlors of townspeople's homes and decorated with apples, flat wafers, sweets and paper roses. The rose was a symbol of the Virgin Mary, and the flat wafers represented the communion symbol for Christ. With its religious significance, this tree became known as *Christbaum*.

In the seventeenth and eighteenth centuries, the *Christbaum* took on many shapes. In Austria and Germany, the tip was cut from large evergreens and hung upside down in a corner of the living room. The tree was then decorated with gilded nuts, red paper and apples.

Though these are the earliest recorded examples of evergreen trees linked with Christmas traditions, flowering and fruit-bearing trees have been associated with the holiday as far back as the tenth century. Legends abound about trees and bushes that mysteriously bloom at Christmas despite the ice and snow of winter. A French legend tells us that on Christmas Eve a giant tree could be seen for miles because it was lighted by candles on each branch. On the top was the Baby Jesus surrounded by a beautiful halo. A legend repeated in Syria by local Christians, recounts how after the Three Wise Men were leaving Bethlehem the trees bent over to show them an alternate route home, which was the safer way. Another legend tells that at midnight on January 5, Epiphany Eve, when the Magi arrived, the trees in Bethlehem bowed reverently.

Another popular and frequently told legend attributes Martin Luther with being the first person to chop down a tree and bring it home for his family's celebration.

Martin Luther was a sixteenth century German monk who was the leader in his country of the Protestant Reformation which questioned certain church practices. One cold, snowy Christmas Eve, he was walking through the forest on his way home. He looked up and saw the stars sparkling down through the snow-covered branches, as if they were a part of the tree itself.

"What a beautiful sight," Martin Luther thought. "The sky must have looked much like this on the first Christmas Eve in Bethlehem. I must share this beauty with my children."

However, the tree was very large and very tall and the night was freezing. There was a lot of snow on the ground, and Luther knew it was much too cold for the children to leave their warm and cozy home. Just then he spotted a tiny fir tree growing beside the tall one.

"I can cut down this little tree with my ax and take it home to my children," he decided. "And, so they can share the beauty I have seen, I will put candles on all the branches and they will sparkle just like the stars that shone on the tree in the forest."

Martin Luther took his ax and carefully cut down the little fir tree. When he arrived home, carrying the small fir, he told his children what he had seen.

"I have brought you this tree which we will decorate with lighted candles to represent the Christ Child as the Light of the World," he told them.

The children were delighted, and when all the candles were lit, his son exclaimed, "They look like stars shining in the sky — like the stars that shown in Bethlehem the night Jesus was born." His daughter placed a *crèche* with figures of Joseph, Mary, the Christ Child and the animals in the manger under the tree.

In the fourteenth and fifteenth centuries, during the Advent season, people in Europe performed miracle or mystery plays in front of cathedrals. Since few people could read the scriptures, this was a convenient means to dramatize and teach Bible stories. In Germany, these were called "Paradise Plays," and in a scene representing the Garden of Eden, a fir tree laden with apples was used to depict the sin of Adam and Eve and their expulsion from paradise. The play ended with the promise of Christ's coming and was a popular pre-Christmas play for many years. Because the tree was the only prop used, its image lasted in the minds of those attending, and possibly influenced the German people to bring trees into their homes at Christmas. The fir tree in the play represented the tree of life, as well as sin, so when people first decorated trees, they began by putting sweets and little religious figures on the branches, signifying their reverence. Germans had been burning candles in pyramid-shaped frames covered with evergreens for years; they simply transferred that custom to the trees.

There is general agreement that the Christmas tree as we know it originated in Germany. Again, as in other cultures, evergreen trees were a sign of life amid the deep, winter cold — an assurance that spring would return. Trees were plentiful, and often each member of the family decorated her own tree for the holiday season. These were small trees which sat on a table, festooned with candles on each branch and surrounded with sweets and gifts.

The tradition became popular, and soon spread to Scandinavian countries where fir trees grew in abundance. Christmas trees did not become a popular part of other European's Christmas celebrations until after the tradition had traveled to America in 1746 with German settlers.

In 1761, the German Princess Charlotte married England's King George III, and brought the German Christmas tree tradition to England. Other German princesses, including Adelaide who married William IV in 1818, continued the tradition.

However, it was German-born Prince Albert and Queen Victoria who popularized the custom when they erected the first Christmas tree in Windsor Castle. The tree delighted their children and everyone who saw it. Because the English loved to imitate the Royal Family, it soon became a popular custom in Britain.

The first known American Christmas trees were decorated for children in Bethlehem, Pennsylvania, which was settled by Moravians. Most residents of

Christmas: Traditions and Legends

Bethlehem brought to America their tradition of small trees placed on tables in the middle of the living room. Because there was an abundance of trees in the eastern United States, cutting a large, full-grown tree was soon the custom.

In the prairies and plains of our country, like Kansas or parts of the Dakotas where there were few trees, children hung stockings on the backs of chairs and decorated tumbleweed or dried sunflower stalks. When the railroad tracks were laid across the United States, trees were transported across the country by trains, which were met with great anticipation and excitement by the children. All the townspeople rushed to the station and loaded their wagons with trees to take home and decorate.

The tradition of a Christmas tree in the White House started in 1856 with President Franklin Pierce. In 1901, when Theodore Roosevelt became President, he tried, rather unsuccessfully, to have them banned. President Roosevelt, a noted conservationist, had been warned that the continued cutting of Christmas trees was going to deplete the forests, so he promptly banned their use in the White House. However, his two sons, Archie and Quentin, smuggled a tree into the White House and set it up in Archie's closet. Fortunately, after being discovered, the boys were able to convince Gifford Pinchot, a noted conservationist, to intervene. He explained to President Roosevelt that thinning the forest by cutting down trees actually helped the trees thrive and survive. Ever since, each administration has continued the custom of having decorated trees in the White House. Between 1923 and 1973, a tree from a different state was brought to the White House each year.

In 1923, President Calvin Coolidge placed a fir tree from his native state of Vermont on the Capitol steps, and the first outdoor lighting ceremony took place. The first Christmas Eve service at the White House was also held in 1923. The custom has continued, and today the entire nation, along with thousands of visitors watch as the President lights the National Community Christmas Tree during an evening ceremony on the west lawn of the White House.

The custom of community Christmas trees is thought to have started in America in 1909, when the townspeople of Pasadena, California, decorated a tree atop Mount Wilson, overlooking the city. Three years later, New York's Madison Square Park erected a sixty-foot balsam fir "Tree of Light," while 20,000 people gathered around the huge tree to sing carols. This custom of singing carols around a community tree spread quickly. In 1913, in Philadelphia's Independence Square, the "Children's Christmas Tree" helped popularize the tradition. Since 1933, Rockefeller Center boasts what many consider America's most beautiful community Christmas tree. It is estimated that it is visited by over two million people each year. This annual tree-lighting ceremony is rivaled only by the tree-lighting ceremony on the White House lawn.

There are many

"Christmas Tree Lane" celebrations throughout the country. A designated area, a street or lane, or a three- or four-block area or neighborhood, is decorated extravagantly by local residents. The first Christmas Tree Lane was opened in Altadena, California, in 1920, and is still going strong. This mile-long avenue is bordered by gigantic, graceful deodar cedars whose seeds were brought from India by Captain Frederick J. Woodbury years ago. More than 10,000 multi-colored lights decorate these magnificent cedars each year, and the unusual and inspiring spectacle has been enjoyed by millions over the years.

The battle for the tallest, the biggest, or the most unusual Christmas tree has been going on for some time. Wilmington, North Carolina, lays claim to the largest living Christmas tree, an oak identified as "more than three hundred years old, with branches that spread 210 feet, and a trunk with a circumference of fourteen feet." It was the first tree decorated with electric lights in 1929 and is trimmed each year with over 7,000 multi-colored bulbs. This task takes eight days to put up the lights, and another eight to take them down. No such claim is made in Troy, Montana, though their ponderosa pine towers a majestic 115 feet into the sky. Oldtimers in the town date the first tree lighting back to 1927. Had it not been for a worker who haphazardly "topped" the tree, it would be much taller. Before the topping, the tree was adding about eighteen inches of growth to its height each year.

Perhaps vying for the most unusual tree, the City of Los Angeles erected a 96-foot white spruce in Pershing Square in 1948. It would be hard to compete with a tree in Minneapolis, Minnesota, in 1947. That tree was sixty-five feet tall and had been constructed by inserting 135 small individual Christmas trees into water pipes that were attached — like spokes on a wheel — to a telephone pole.

In 1948, the townspeople of Bellingham, Washington, celebrated Christmas around a Douglas fir 134 feet high, and then outdid themselves in 1949 with one 153 feet tall. This tree was felled near Sumas, which is only about twenty miles from Bellingham, and it took two logging trucks three days to deliver it.

The city wired the lights in such a manner that Edward R. Murrow, who grew up nearby, could turn them on from New York City. Two years later, in nearby Seattle, a shopping center raised a tree which set the record for the tallest Christmas tree. It was 212 feet high and weighed in at 25 tons.

The "Nation's Christmas Tree" is a magnificent giant sequoia redwood located in Kings Canyon National Park in Sanger, California. The ancient tree is an estimated 2,000 years old and has grown to a height of 267 feet. Named after General Grant, it was discovered in 1924 when a group of friends were visiting the park. A little girl wandered away from the adults, and when found, she was staring up in awe at this incredible sight. When the group approached, the little girl stood there for a moment in silence, then exclaimed, "What a beautiful Christmas tree that would be."

The tree was designated the Nation's Christmas Tree on April 28, 1926. Each year on the second Sunday in December, a caravan starts in Sanger and proceeds into the Sierra Mountains to hold a nondenominational service at the base of the tree. When snow conditions make it impossible to reach the tree, the service is held nearby, with any willing visitors making the trek to place a wreath at the base of the tree.

It is apparent that this cherished tradition of celebrating Christ's birth around a decorated tree is one of the most popular and beloved parts of our Christmas season. Many of us remember when we were children and how exciting it was to pick out the family Christmas tree. People say one of the first considerations in buying a home is "where will the Christmas tree go?" Of all the customs associated with this holiday, the tree aglow with lights and spangled decorations creates more childhood memories than perhaps anything else except the Christmas Eve visitor. You know, the one with the red suit, the white beard and the reindeer.

To help us appreciate the variety of trees we have in this country, think about this — in India they have an abundance of banana trees — so you know what they do? They place ornaments on bananas.

"Leave a peppermint stick for old Saint Nick,
hanging on the Christmas tree...."

A Christmas Tree Legend

In a small cottage in the middle of a great forest, there lived a poor woodcutter and his family. Each morning, they rose early and cut wood to earn money for food and clothing. The woodcutter, his wife, and their two children all worked very hard, but they still did not make enough to take care of their most meager needs. It did not seem to matter, as they were a happy family and the children were always cheerful. Theirs was a very loving and caring home.

One Christmas Eve, the family sat around the fireplace eating their simple supper. There was a fierce storm outside and a dark wind hurled snow around the cottage. In the midst of the storm the mother thought she heard a knock on the door.

"Who could be coming to see us on such a cold, bitter night?" she asked.

The woodcutter opened the door and found a small child, pale, tired and shivering. His clothes were torn and ragged. In a forlorn voice, the child said, "I am a poor child who has nothing to eat and no place to go. Please let me come in."

"Of course, dear child, do come in," the woodcutter said. "We do not have much food, but you are most welcome to share what we have. Here, come over by the fire and warm yourself. It is bitter cold out there."

The child quickly ate the food they had left, and when he finished, the woodcutter's wife spoke: "You must be very tired. I'll bet you would like to go to bed now."

The children, almost in unison, told the child, "You may sleep in my bed."

Their guest was immediately sound asleep on a cozy cot by the fireplace.

The children spent the night wrapped in blankets near the fireplace, and together they prayed to God, thanking him for their warm and safe home. The little stranger had only heaven for a roof and the cold earth for a bed. They had parents who loved and took care of them. They fell asleep with grateful hearts.

In the early morning of the next day, the children were suddenly awakened. At first, they were not sure what had happened. Then their parents joined them, and they all listened to the most beautiful singing they had ever heard. It seemed to be coming from outside the house. They all ran to the window and looked out. The orphaned child who had appeared the night before was standing in the snow with a choir of angels surrounding him, singing a lovely Christmas carol.

The child was no longer wearing the tattered rags He had arrived in. He was costumed in magnificent robes and was surrounded by a glowing, sparkling light. His arms stretched upwards towards the heavens.

The woodcutter and his family went outside so they could see better. When the child saw them, He walked to where they stood, then said, "I am the Christ Child, bringing happiness to good children. I have gladly received your kindness, your gift of love, and now this is my gift to you."

He broke a branch from a small fir tree and planted it in the ground by the door of the cottage. "Behold," He told them, "here is my gift. From this day forward, this tree shall bear its fruit at Christmas, and you shall always have plenty, even in the dead of winter. This shall be a sign of your goodness to me and of faith that shall never die."

As they stood listening to the Christ Child, the branch grew into a tree covered with nuts, lights, fruit, and threads of gold. It was the most magnificent sight they had ever seen.

The Fir Tree

Adapted from Hans Christian Andersen

The little fir tree lived in the deep woods. It was a lovely place to live with lots of sunshine and fresh air, and all kinds of larger trees as neighbors. Often, the peasant children came by looking for berries to pick, and they would sit down by the little fir tree and say, "What a pretty little tree this is." That is not what the fir tree wanted to hear. What he wanted most of all was to be a big tree like all the others.

"If only I could be as great and tall as the rest of the trees," he sighed. "I could spread my branches way out, and see the world from my top, birds would build nests in my boughs, and I could bend ever so gracefully in the wind."

He found no pleasure in the sunshine, the birds or the clouds above him, and did not understand when a sunbeam said to him, "Little fir tree, you should rejoice in your youth, for you will grow bigger and stronger soon enough."

"Oh, but I want to grow and grow and become older and taller. That is the most wonderful thing in the world."

In the wintertime, when the ground was covered with glittering snow, a hare often came by and leapt right over the fir tree. That really angered him. Two winters passed, and when the third arrived, the tree had finally grown so much that the hare had to go around it. This pleased the fir, but he was still not as big as he wished.

Each winter, woodcutters came and felled some of the larger trees in the forest. When they came again this year, the fir tree, which by now had grown to a respectable size, trembled as he watched the magnificent trees fall to the ground with a resounding crash. Then their branches were stripped off, and the bare trees were laid in wagons and hauled away. The little fir tree had no idea where the naked trees were going or what would become of them.

When the stork and the swallows returned in the spring, the tree asked them, "Do you know where they took the trees? Did you see them anywhere?"

The swallows replied that they knew nothing, but the stork said, "I think I know. When I left Egypt, I flew over many ships that had magnificent masts that smelled like fir. I believe the masts were made from those trees. They were very impressive, I can tell you."

"Oh, how I hope I will grow big and tall enough to go out to sea. What does the sea look like?" asked the tree.

"That is too hard to explain, " replied the stork and flew away.

"Rejoice in your growth," the sunbeams

urged. "Rejoice in your new growth, and in the new life it brings."

And the wind kissed the tree and the dew wept tears on its branches, but still the fir tree did not understand.

At Christmas time, the woodcutters cut down much younger trees, some even younger and smaller than the fir. The fir tree, ever restless, always yearning to leave the forest, was very puzzled and disappointed that he still was not chosen. He asked, "Where are they going? They are not taller than I. In fact, one of them is much smaller, and none of them have their branches stripped. Where are they being taken?"

"We know," chirped the sparrows. "We know where they are going, because we have seen them in the windows in town. They are taken into warm houses, placed in the middle of the room and covered with the most splendid things you can imagine — apples, honey cakes, toys and hundreds of candles. They are called Christmas trees."

"Then what happens to them?" the fir tree asked, trembling.

"We do not know. That is all we saw, but it was incredibly beautiful."

"Oh, how I long to be one of those Christmas trees. It would be even grander than going to sea. I am tall now and my branches spread like those that were chosen last year. I want to be on the cart where someone will choose me and put me in a warm room, then cover my branches with glorious ornaments. For after that, surely something even grander and more wonderful will happen, otherwise why would they adorn me so? Oh, why do I suffer such longing — what is the matter with me?"

Though the tree grew and grew all year, he did not rejoice. He stood in the forest in his dark green splendor, and people who saw him, remarked on what a fine tree he was. Then Christmas came, and he was the first tree to be cut. The axe struck deep into him, and when he fell to the ground, it was with a sigh. Yet, the happiness he expected did not come. Instead, he thought of his friends — the sunshine, the clouds, the birds, all the bushes and flowers he had grown up with, and a pang of sorrow filled his heart.

He was still thinking about having to leave his home when he realized the wagon had arrived at the yard. All the trees were unloaded, and the fir had just been propped up against a fence when he heard a man say, "This one is perfect. We don't even need to look at any others." Two servants arrived in a livery and carried him into a beautiful drawing room filled with portraits, silken sofas, easy chairs, Chinese vases, large tables of picture-books and toys worth hundreds of dollars — or so the children had said. The fir tree was placed in a sand-filled tub which was covered with a green cloth. The tree trembled in anticipation.

Everyone, including the servants, began to decorate his branches. They hung little nets cut out of colored paper and filled with sweets; they suspended walnuts and gilded apples; they placed dolls and toy soldiers among the foliage, and blue and white tapered candles were fastened to the tree's boughs. The top of the tree shimmered with a star of gold tinsel. It was splendid, unbelievably splendid.

"This evening," the young ladies proclaimed, "our tree will shine and shine." The tree did not know how he would be able to wait that long. He wondered what would happen next. Would all the other trees in the forest come to admire him? Would the sparrows peek through the windows? Would he take root in the sand and remain there winter and summer adorned with ornaments?

All this wondering gave the tree a backache, which is as bad for a tree as a headache is for a person.

Later that evening, candles were lighted and brought about such brilliance the tree trembled in every bough, which caused one candle to fall and set fire to the foliage. The fire was quickly put out, but the tree knew he dared not tremble again. He was quite bewildered by the bright flames. Then the parlor doors opened and the children rushed into the room. They danced around the tree, pulling presents from it. The children rushed around so gleefully the tree's branches creaked and he feared he would fall down.

"Oh, what is to happen now?" he thought. By then the candles had burned down to the branches and had to be put out. When the last one was extinguished, the children were given permission to plunder the tree. They rushed toward him and fell on him so hard his branches cracked. If the star on the top had not been fastened to the ceiling, he would surely have fallen over.

"A story! We want you to tell us a story," the children shouted as they pulled a little fat man toward the tree. He sat down near the tree and proclaimed, "You must choose the story, for I will tell only one. The tree can listen, too."

There was a babble of shouting the names of stories, and the fir tree thought, "Shouldn't I be able to shout with the rest? Am I to do nothing?" But he had been part of the evening's entertainment and had done what was expected of him.

The fat man told the story of Klumpey-Dumpey, who tumbled down, nevertheless had gained the crown and married a princess. The children clapped their hands, and the tree thought he had never heard a lovelier story. Never had the birds in the woods told a story like this. If Klumpey-Dumpey could fall down and end up marrying a princess, surely he, too, would live happily ever after. He would look forward to the next evening when he would be adorned again with candles, toys and fruit.

"I will not tremble tomorrow. I will hear another lovely story and rejoice in all my splendor," the tree thought, and stood still all night thinking of his wonderful future.

The next morning, the servants came into the parlor. "Now I will be decorated anew," thought the tree. But the servants grabbed his trunk and dragged him out of the room, up some stairs to an attic, stuffing him into a dark corner where they left him. The tree was devastated. "What are they doing to me? Why are they leaving me here?" thought the tree. He leaned against the wall contemplating his fate.

Days and nights passed and no one came into the attic. It seemed he had been completely forgotten and the tree did not understand why. Finally he decided that he had been placed in the attic to protect him until spring. "How thoughtful and considerate," he thought, "I just wish it wasn't so lonely and dark in here. It was so pleasant in the woods with the snow on the ground, and I would even welcome the hare if he came to visit. It is really terribly lonely here."

"Squeak, squeak," a little mouse said, peeking out of his hole. He crept toward the fir tree, followed closely by a second mouse. They sniffed around him and climbed up on his branches.

"It is very cold in here," said the first mouse. "Otherwise it would be most comfortable. Don't you agree, old tree?"

"I am not old!" the fir responded indignantly. "There are many trees a lot older than I."

"Where are you from, and why are you here?" asked the second mouse. "Can you tell us about the most beautiful spot on earth? Have you visited the storeroom, where cheeses lay on the shelf, where hams hang, and where you go in lean and come out fat?" They were extremely curious.

"I do not know of this place," the tree replied. "But, I do know the woods where the birds sing, the sun shines and it is very beautiful." Then he told the mice about his youth, and since they had never before heard anything like that, they listened intently, then said, "You must have been *so* happy then."

"Well," the tree said thoughtfully, "yes, I guess I was quite happy." He then told the mice about Christmas Eve, when he was bedecked with all those wonderful ornaments.

"Oh, what a wonderful story. You have indeed been fortunate, old fir tree."

"I am not that old," the fir said. "I just came out of the woods and am in my prime, but I am kind of short for my age."

"You know some marvelous stories." the mice told him.

The next night when they arrived, they were accompanied by four other little mice who had come to hear the tree tell his stories. The more the fir tree recalled his life in the woods, the more he realized what happy times those had been. Then he remembered how Klumpey-Dumpey fell down and still married a princess. "Those happy days may come again," he said. "Perhaps I, too, will marry a princess like Klumpey-Dumpey did."

"Who is Klumpey-Dumpey?" the mice asked. So the fir told them the entire fairy tale which he remembered word for word, and the mice were so thrilled, they jumped to the top of the tree.

The next evening many more mice came and two rats joined them the following night. The rats said they did not find the story interesting, and this made the mice sad, but they were also becoming tired of the same tale.

"I only know that one," the tree replied. "It is the one I heard on the happiest night of my life. I just didn't know how happy I was."

"It is a ridiculous story. Don't you know any stories about the larder or candles?"

"No," the tree said sadly.

"Then we do not want to visit you again," the rats declared. Eventually, the mice stopped coming also and the fir tree was alone again.

"It was very nice when the little mice came to see me and listened when I spoke. But that is over, too. I will just have to take care of myself until someone comes to take me out of this place. I will be so happy that day," sighed the tree.

Finally, one morning, people came and began working in the attic. They moved trunks and pulled the tree from the corner, then threw him down hard on the floor. One of the servants picked the tree up and took him to the stairway where the sunlight shone.

"Now my life will begin again," the tree thought. He could feel the fresh air and see the sunbeams as he was carried out to the courtyard. Things had happened so fast, he didn't even think about how he looked. The garden nearby was lovely with blossoming trees and fragrant roses. He tried to spread out his branches but they were brown and brittle. He lay in a corner among nettles and weeds. The gold tinsel star still sat on his top and glistened in the sun. Some of the children who had helped decorate the fir tree on Christmas Eve were playing in the courtyard, and one of them grabbed the star and tore it from his top.

"Look what an ugly old tree this is," another child said, and jumped and down on the branches until they all cracked under his feet.

The fir tree looked around him at all the beautiful flowers and trees, then saw what had become of him, and wished he had stayed in the corner in the attic. He thought of when he was young in the woods, of the merry Christmas Eve and of the little mice who had loved his story of Klumpey-Dumpey.

"The past! The past! Why couldn't I rejoice when I had reason to?" he wondered.

Then the gardener's son came over with an ax and chopped the fir into little pieces. A servant lit a match and set fire to the bundle on the ground. The tree blazed brightly and sighed deeply, thinking how foolish he had been. Each sigh was like a shot.

The children played in the garden, and the little boy wore the star on his chest — the star which the tree had worn on his happiest evening. Now, that was all over, the tree's life was all over, and the story is all over.

Legend of the Fir Tree

On the night of the Christ Child's birth, all living creatures heard the good news and went to Bethlehem to honor Him and bring Him gifts. Even the trees in the forest wanted to go and give Him something special.

"I can give Him some of my olives," said the olive tree.

"And I will give Him all the dates He wants," the date tree promised.

The little fir tree was sad, as he had nothing to offer but his needles, and they would surely prick the little Babe. Besides, he was tired from the long journey and could hardly stand. The bigger trees pushed and shoved until he was almost completely hidden in the background.

An angel was watching and saw the little fir tree looking unhappy. In fact, he was *so* sad and *so* tired, he started crying. That only made things worse, and the little tree was so embarrassed, he began to move further and further back, thinking he should just leave altogether.

The angel, seeing all this, looked up at the stars in the heavens, calling to them, "Please come down and sit on the little fir tree's branches so he can be beautiful for the Christ Child. Then he will stay to honor Him."

The stars were most happy to come down, so they, too, could visit the Holy Child. When they nestled among the little fir tree's branches, they tickled him and he giggled. All the other trees turned to look, and the fir tree sparkled and twinkled so brightly, he lit up everything around him. In a single movement, all the other trees parted to make a pathway for him. He marched proudly past all of them, making his way to the manger.

When the Christ Child saw the little fir tree, glittering from top to bottom, His face lit up at such a lovely sight, and He smiled.

"What a pretty tree you are," He said. "I bless you and promise that at Christmas forevermore fir trees will be lighted to please all the children in the world."

That is how the fir tree came to be a very special Christmas tree.

The Fire Is So Delightful

The ritual of the Yule Log Ceremony has deep pagan roots, having been a celebration of the sun among the Celts, Teutons and Druids. They believed the sun stood still for twelve days at the end of the year, and fearing the sun might stop forever, pagans dragged a huge log from the woods, put it in the center of the town square and lit it as a symbol of keeping the sun alive.

The fire was a source of light and heat during the darkest days. The log had to be large enough to burn for twelve days, for it was believed that only then would the evil spirits be driven away and the sun's return be assured. Sometimes the log was a whole tree trunk, roots and all, and was so large it had to be pulled by oxen.

Peasants in northern Europe had a feast called Yule, where they brought a big log into the home on Christmas Eve. They couldn't buy the log — it had to come from their own land. The entire family participated in choosing and hauling in the log. It was a joyous occasion, especially among the children, who decorated the log with greenery and ribbons and sang cheerful songs on the way home. The peasants also feared the sun would die and believed the burning log kept it alive.

In some rural areas of France, families gathered for their Great Supper on Christmas Eve, which included "laying the Yule Log." After everyone attended Mass, they returned home and gathered in the kitchen. The oldest family member, representing the year past, and the youngest family member, representing the year coming, laid the log in the fireplace; the oldest member lifted a cup of wine and poured part of it on the log three times.

"In the name of the Father, the Son and the Holy Ghost," he said, emptying his cup. Then he stood and chanted, "Burn, Yule Log, burn," and everyone responded, "Joy! Joy!" and the Great Supper would begin.

In Scandinavia, a log was burned to honor

Christmas: Traditions and Legends

Thor, their god of thunder, whom they believed protected their homes from thunder and lightning. Germans burned their log for only a short time, then stored it in a safe place. Whenever there was a thunderstorm during the next year, the people put the remaining piece in the fireplace, believing lightning would not strike a home where a yule log was burning. The French soaked the log in water, which they fed to their cows, confident they would produce more calves. Some people hoped the ghosts of their ancestors would come and get warm by the heat of the log.

Though the superstition surrounding the Yule Log varied from country to country, the Yule Log ceremony had several similarities. The English version was probably the simplest. Returning home with the log, everyone paraded around the kitchen three times before laying the log in the fireplace. The one who lit the log must have clean hands, as unwashed hands prevented the log from burning. It was considered bad luck to light the log before Christmas Eve, or to let the fire go out for the next twelve days.

When the church bells were heard on Christmas Eve, the ceremony began as the family members gathered. An important part of the ritual was to light the fire with a piece of last year's log. The log was sprinkled with holy water, then blessed in the name of the Holy Trinity. The father then poured wine on the log three times, and a prayer was offered so that the fire might warm the cold, that the hungry might find food, the weary enjoy rest, and everyone experience heaven's peace.

After the log was lit, games were played around the fireplace, and the children danced and sang songs. Later, they told ghost stories, drank cider and watched their shadows flicker on the wall until the church bells announced the midnight hour, which was bedtime.

Small pieces of the log were carried to bed to guard against evil spirits. When the holiday was over, a piece of partially burned log was saved to start next year's fire, and stored in the house as protection against fire and lightning in the coming year. Ashes were taken outside and spread around fruit trees to help them bear fruit; some thought the ashes had healing powers which cured diseases of men and animals.

The Yule Log ceremony was an integral part of past Christmas celebrations and continues to this day in some English homes. To delight guests every Christmas, the Empress Hotel in Victoria, British Columbia, Canada, holds a Yule Log lighting ceremony. Since 1927, the Ahwahnee Hotel in Yosemite National Park has recreated the Bracebridge Dinner for their guests. The Yule Log ceremony, traditionally presented on Christmas Eve in the Great Lounge of the hotel, is part of this celebration. The log burns throughout the holiday season.

Palmer Lake, Colorado, has an annual Yule Log hunt, which, except for the war years, has been held since 1933. Prior to the Sunday before Christmas, a log is cut, notched, and hidden in the woods. On that Sunday, at an appointed time, a trumpet sounds and all who wish to participate gather at the Town Hall to search the woods. The hunters, wearing red and green hats, follow leaders past the Little Log Church, through Vail Gulch, and up Sundance Peak. When people approach the spot near the hidden log, a signal is given, and they are on their own to find the log, which has a rope around it. Whoever finds the Yule Log climbs on top of it and rides it back to town, carried by the others. That lucky person also gets the first cup of wassail, a special ale, at the celebration which takes place in the Town Hall when all return. The Yule Log is then cut in half, with one half placed on kindling from last year's fire, and the other half saved as the kindling log for next year. This ritual has become such a popular tradition that hundreds of splinters from the log have been sent to other communities who want to start their own Yule Log celebration.

In most other parts of America, we celebrate the Yule Log ceremony by the tradition of eating a Yule Log cake, which is believed to have originated in France, since there was a dearth of fireplaces in French cities. French chefs created special cakes, shaped like a log and covered with chocolate icing to resemble bark on a tree and decorated with meringue mushrooms. In the United States, we add holly leaves and berries made of frosting to the delicious cake.

The Yule Log created fire, a symbol of safety and home to ancient people, and often was the only source of light after the sun went down. Christians believed the flame of the Yule Log signified the light that came from heaven when Christ was born. Even today, a fire in the fireplace, especially at Christmastime, creates a warm and cozy feeling.

"Let it snow, let it snow, let it snow...."

It's Beginning To Look A Lot Like Christmas

Regardless of how full and beautiful or how sparse and spindly our tree may be, the delicious task of decorating it usually transforms any tree into something magical: a Christmas tree. Ornaments hide the many flaws, taking an ordinary tree and changing it into one we all "oooh and aaah" over. Excitement mounts as family members retrieve the familiar boxes from the basement, attic or garage, and everyone starts unwrapping the treasures gathered over the years. Decorating the tree is one of the best Christmas traditions, one which may include playing favorite Christmas music, sipping an eggnog, building a fire in the fireplace, and getting the whole family involved. The size of the family changes over the years, but our memories remain; and when we unwrap those beloved ornaments, it's easy to slip back in time and remember when we were children or when our children were small.

The original Christmas decorations were usually associated with or tied to pagan beliefs. In the Scandinavian countries, people made decorations out of straw and fashioned them in the shape of stars, crowns, angels and even billy goats. They believed that straw and wheat were magical and brought good luck.

Several of the decorations of the early Christians honored the birth of Jesus. Animals carved out of wood reminded them of those in the stable at Bethlehem. A star on the top of the tree represented the star which led the Wise Men to the Christ Child.

In the Middle Ages, Germans and Italians displayed light wooden frames shaped like a pyramid. These consisted of several tiers of shelves which were decorated with evergreens, candles and trinkets. In Germany, this Christmas pyramid was called a *lichstock*, and served as a candelabra. It was known as a *ceppo* in Italy, and frequently had a *presipio* (manger) at the bottom where small gifts were placed. The traditions of the trees in paradise plays, the *Christbaum,* the *Lichstock* and *ceppo* all came together late in the sixteenth century when the first decorated trees appeared in Germany.

Some trees were decorated with only sweets, nuts and fruit, and were called sugar trees. In some countries, on January 6, the Twelfth Night, the children dismantled the tree and ate all the decorations. In other countries, the tree was decorated with presents; when the children came down on

Christmas morning, they completely stripped the tree.

Many of the early decorations were handmade. People made cookies in the shapes of Christmas symbols and hung painted nuts and fruit on the trees. Children made paper chains and paper angels with cotton wings and paper ribbons. Eggshells, carefully broken in two and colored, became tiny baskets which could be filled with candies. The practice soon spread throughout Europe and America. Early North American trees were trimmed with good things to eat — imitating the European trees. Americans added strings of popcorn and cranberries sometime in the 1860s. Hanging caramelized popcorn balls was also popular. Some people used food coloring to produce red and green popcorn chains. The candy cane, which once represented a shepherd's crook in Europe and was easy to hang on the tree, became a favorite decoration in America.

When handmade ornaments became too heavy to hang on trees, German glass blowers began to manufacture the first glass ornaments, which were originally imported to America in the 1870s. Lauscha, a village in Germany, was the primary manufacturer of glass ornaments prior to 1939. Glass blowers in this village became so skilled they could form tiny teapots and attach miniature spouts and handles to them, as well as trumpets which produced a note and bells that actually rang. After the Second World War, the village became part of East Germany, and the art was lost to American production lines. In 1939, Corning Glass Company began making glass ornaments in the United States using machinery which produced more ornaments in one minute than the German glass blowers made in a day.

After it became obvious that lighted candles on trees were far too dangerous, electric lights replaced them. The first electric lights used on a Christmas tree were custom-made, appropriately enough, for the president of Edison Electric Company. The year was 1882, three years after Thomas Edison first demonstrated the electric bulb. The string consisted of eighty bulbs blinking in red, white and blue. People were immediately captivated by this invention, but only wealthy families could afford them. In fact, it was necessary to hire an electrician to hand-wire the tree at a cost equal to $2,000 today.

The first ready-made string of twenty-eight lights in the United States was made around 1903 and cost $12, an average man's weekly pay. When one light burned out, they all went out, and it was a long, hard search in, under and over ornaments and branches to find the bad bulb. It is hard to imagine decorating a Christmas tree without lights; whether we choose one color or many, blinking or non-blinking, big or small, inside or out, lights are now part of Christmas.

Cities across America have Christmas displays that have become as traditional as trees and Santa Claus. For more than seventy-five years, citizens of Altadena, California, have decorated their Christmas Tree Lane, a mile-long avenue hung with over 500 separate strings of 10,000 lights. A switch-on ceremony is held December 10, and "the oldest large-scale outdoor light display in the world" stays lighted until New Year's Day.

What started out with a single strand of lights over a store entrance in 1925, has evolved into one of the most spectacular lighting displays in the country. On Thanksgiving evening, Country Club Plaza in Kansas City, Missouri, fills with thousands of people who come to observe the annual "flip-of-the-switch" ceremony, which turns on over 200,000 lights. The display illuminates a fourteen-block area of the Plaza, and the lights outline every tower, balcony, dome, courtyard and building. Horse-drawn carriages carry passengers past holiday-decorated windows, and carolers fill the air with Christmas songs.

Portland, Oregon, has Peacock Lane, a residential area consisting of thirty-three homes in a four-block area. Decorating for Christmas began in 1929, was halted during World War II, and resumed in 1948. Each year, prior to Christmas, these homeowners spend countless hours decorating their homes with thousands of lights, nativity scenes, Santa Clauses, and lighted trees, both inside and outside. Every night for three weeks, they observe chattering groups of visitors who line the streets admiring their handiwork. Many cities have displays which may not be quite as spectacular, but they are all appreciated, especially by children of all ages. Being a visitor in another city at Christmas makes one realize what a universal custom it is to have winking and blinking lights decorating town squares, department stores and trees along sidewalks.

Some interesting decorations have been noted over the years. In 1893, a New York importer named Amos M. Lyon included in his Christmas catalog, miniature pieces of kitchen equipment — bottles, rolling pins and inch-high potato mashers. One family, having no money to buy decorations, simply hung all their knives, forks and spoons on the tree. At the opposite end was James Clements, who, in 1897, decorated his tree with $70,000 worth of gold nuggets from the Klondike Gold Rush!

Some of us have special ornaments we decorate with each year. Maybe they have been handed down for generations, were made by one of our children, or were a special gift or souvenir. Regardless of their origin, each year when we place these precious ornaments on the fragrant boughs of our tree, it's like finding old friends. After years of use they may no longer be bright and shiny, but when we unwrap these time-honored treasures, and they take their place among the green branches, our memories come out of storage as well. Another Christmas, another beautiful tree.

"We wish you a Merry Christmas...."

The Legend Of Icicles

It was wintertime, and as night fell, the forest was becoming very cold and dark. The wind howled fiercely through the branches of the trees, and snow blanketed the path the Christ Child walked on. Shivering from the piercing cold, the weary Christ Child knew night would soon be descending.

"I must find a place to sleep," He thought. "But where?"

He had been wandering for hours and did not know this part of the forest. When He looked around, all the trees were bare, for their branches had long since lost their leaves. He needed someplace to shelter Himself from the bitter night, where He could lie down and be safe and warm. He looked in every direction yet could not find any refuge.

Just then, a cloud moved and covered the moon, making it difficult to see. To make matters worse, snow began to fall more thickly. The Christ Child knew He could not make His legs move much farther. He stood in the middle of the forest trembling.

Suddenly the moon peered out from behind the cloud, and it was almost as bright as day. And there, right in front of Him, was a big, lovely pine tree, whose branches were long and bushy and draped over the ground like a tent.

"This beautiful tree will shelter me from the storm," He said gratefully. "I will crawl under its branches and be quite safe from the wind and frost." He snuggled in under the pine tree, warm and cozy and secure. Soon He was fast asleep.

The next morning, as soon as it was light, the pine tree awakened and saw the Christ Child asleep under its branches. The storm had passed, and the tree realized it had been a haven for the Little Child. Tears of happiness and pride began to fall on its branches and, as they fell, they miraculously turned into icicles. When the sun came out and shone on the icicles, the pine tree sparkled and glistened and twinkled so brightly it lit up the entire forest.

Just then, the Christ Child awoke and, looking at the shimmering pine tree, said, "Thank you, dear tree, for saving me from the bitter storm. You are truly the most beautiful tree in the forest." The pine tree bowed his top branch and sighed gratefully, for he was much too surprised to speak.

The next time *you* see an icicle, remember the pine tree's tears of joy; and when the sun shines on the icicle, think about how proud he was when the icicles on his branches sparkled for the Christ Child.

The Legend Of Tinsel

A baby spider woke up, rubbed his eyes, and looked around. It was early Christmas morning, and the house was still. The room was dark except for the light coming from the coals in the fireplace. The spider was disappointed because he had planned for a long time to see the Christmas tree being decorated, but he had been *so* tired, he had fallen asleep. For months, his brother and sister had been telling him how beautiful the Christmas tree would be and how they always stayed up Christmas Eve to watch all the ornaments being placed on the branches. This was his very first Christmas, and he had fallen asleep.

The little spider was sad, he was very sad indeed. "Oh, I want to see, I want to see, I *have* to see that pretty tree!" he said out loud. Then he thought, "Maybe there is enough light for me to see the beautiful ornaments if I just crawl closer. Mommy and Daddy are asleep, and I know my brother and sister are too tired to wake up." They had surely stayed awake to see all the pretty toys and ornaments he knew were on the tree.

The little spider stole across the floor and soon found himself under one of the lower branches. It was hanging on the floor and easy for him to climb on. Suddenly, he felt a smooth, shiny surface under his legs. He was crawling on the biggest, most beautiful, bright, shiny red ornament he could imagine. His brother and sister had tried to describe these wonderful trinkets on the tree, but he had never believed anything could be so splendid.

"Oh, this is *so* much prettier than anything I *ever* dreamed of!" he said to no one. "I must see *everything!*"

He climbed onto the next branch, and there was a magnificent rocking horse with a little boy sitting on top. "This is the most fun I have *ever* had," thought the spider, as he sat on the horse next to the little boy. "But I must hurry because this is such a big tree, and it will soon be time for the children to wake up."

He tried to hurry, but everything was so new and exciting, he was still exploring as dawn came. By this time, the little spider had traveled to almost *all* the branches, and each new decoration was more wondrous than the last. Finally he scurried back down to the bottom for one last peek.

The little spider could not believe his eyes! He had crawled all the way around the tree, and the *entire* tree appeared to be covered with his cobwebs. Every branch he had crawled on and all the spaces in between were a solid mass of the little spider's webs, and he *knew* cobwebs did not belong on a Christmas tree.

"Oh dear, Mommy and Daddy will be very upset with me for climbing on the tree without their permission. I shall never get to see another decorated tree on Christmas Eve." And he began to cry.

Then the baby spider heard a noise, and a bright light appeared in the room. The spider did not know what to do he was so frightened. He started to crawl backwards toward home, but since it was the first time he had ever tried to go any direction but forward, he promptly fell down.

The Christ Child, who had come to bless the Christmas tree, saw the little spider and said to him, "Don't be afraid. I have come to bless the tree." He turned to look at the tree, then turned back to the spider. "My, what lovely cobwebs. You must have worked very hard to make them."

The spider was no longer frightened; in fact, he began to feel rather proud. He giggled to himself at what the Christ Child said, though, because he knew he had not worked at all — he'd had the *best* time of his whole life.

"But," the Christ Child continued, "the webs might frighten the children when they come down. I will turn them into something beautiful."

He walked to the tree and touched each branch. As He did, the cobwebs turned into shiny, sparkling silver tinsel! The spider could hardly believe his eyes, it was so *magnificent*.

But, it had been a very busy and exciting night and he was *so* tired, he could barely keep his eyes open. And, even though his legs were weak and wobbly from all that climbing, he scurried home as quickly as they could carry him. Then he snuggled into bed and immediately fell asleep.

When the children came down on Christmas morning, their eyes were wide with anticipation. The *entire room* shone and twinkled from the glistening silver tinsel. They exclaimed, "This is the *best* Christmas tree we have *ever* had!

Neither their mother nor their father told them they had not put the tinsel on the tree. Somehow, they knew it must be a special surprise for everyone — maybe, even a miracle.

X

I'll Be Home for Christmas

The Legend Of Christ Child And Yule Dough

Joseph, the father of Jesus, learned in a dream that King Herod ordered all boys under the age of two to be slain. He knew that he, Mary, and the Baby Jesus must leave for safety in Egypt immediately. Egypt was a long distance from Jerusalem, and the journey was extremely tiring for the Holy Family. One day they stopped in a village to rest. Joseph knew King Herod's soldiers were not far behind, so he guided Mary and the Tiny Babe toward the shelter of a tree, thinking maybe they could take refuge behind it if the soldiers came before they finished resting.

One of the villagers, a man known for his kindness, was watching the Holy Family and walked over to them.

"You look very tired and frightened," he said to Joseph. "Is something wrong?" Joseph replied, "My family and I must go to Egypt as soon as possible. King Herod has ordered all boys under the age of two slain, and we have a newborn Son."

"Then you shall rest in my home, where you will be safe," he told Joseph, and the Holy Family followed him into his home. What the villager did not realize was that the soldiers would search every home in the village for the Holy Family.

The villager's wife had been kneading dough for bread when Joseph and his family entered their home. They had barely arrived when the sound of horses' hoofs could be heard outside their door.

Mary picked up the Little Babe and held Him toward the villager's wife. "Quick, hide the Baby, for the soldiers must not find Him," she pleaded. The woman took the Babe and dropped Him into the dough just as the soldiers pounded on the door.

The soldiers stomped into the house and demanded to know if they had seen a baby boy traveling through the village. The woman kept her head down and kept kneading and pounding the dough. The villager told the soldiers they had not seen anyone passing through. Mary and Joseph trembled in fear that Jesus would cry out, as the woman was surely slapping Him as she shaped the dough. Not a sound came from the Babe and, after thoroughly searching the house, the soldiers left.

The Holy Family was safe. Mary gently lifted her Son from the dough and, after thanking the villager and his wife for saving their Son's life, Joseph and Mary continued on their journey to Egypt.

When the woman decided to bake her bread, a miraculous thing happened. As soon as Mary had lifted the Little Babe out of the dough, it began to rise. No one noticed it while the Holy Family was leaving, but when the woman turned her attention back to her baking, she noticed that the dough had risen higher and higher until it was light as a feather. The villager's wife baked the bread in her oven, and when she took it out and looked in the dough bowl, there was still some of the rising left in it. No matter how carefully she cleaned it to bake the next batch of bread, there was more dough in the bowl.

Word of this miracle spread throughout the land, and people came from miles away to get a piece of this magical rising to bake with their bread. This started a custom of keeping a small amount of dough for the next rising. Perhaps, too, it started the phrase about bread being the "staff of life," since it is baked and eaten in some form in most cultures. It may also account for our prayer, "Give us this day our daily bread," which symbolizes all food.

I'll Be Home For Christmas

Who can resist? We'll all go on a diet January 1. In the meantime, let's enjoy the delectable holiday treats which appear in front of us wherever we go during the Yuletide Season.

Of all the traditions inherited and adopted by Americans, the foods of Christmas are likely enjoyed by most. Baking all the irresistible cookies, breads, fruitcakes, pies and candies fills the house with wonderful smells for weeks before the holiday arrives. We can thank Sweden for those flaky spritz cookies topped with green and red sugar crystals; Scotland contributed shortbread and marzipan; from England came plum pudding; the French gave us the Yule Log cake; Norway originated the Christmas buns; *lebkuchen* and *springerle* are favorite German cookies. *Lebkuchen* is a spicy, cake-like honey cookie which must age at least three weeks before becoming soft and chewy. Breads such as Germany's *stollen* or Russia's *krendl* are holiday delights especially when decorated with frosting, nuts, candies and Christmas greenery. Cranberry nut, date nut and orange spice are just a few of the delicious varieties of Christmas breads and coffee cakes that most Europeans continued to bake when they came to the United States. Bread molds are used to create a variety of Christmas shapes, such as wreaths, animals, teddy bears and baskets with woven handles which are filled with pastry fruits and vegetables.

It doesn't really matter where these delicious treasures originated as long as they are plentiful during the holidays. Many of us can remember visiting grandparents at Christmastime and heading straight for the cookie jar or pantry. There you would find a treasure-trove of wonderful treats waiting for your indulgence.

Many of the Christmas sweets are enjoyed nationally, others are more popular in certain regions of the United States. Cranberry pie is a favorite in New England, while sweet potato and pecan pies are especially popular in the South. Sugar cookies are made and enjoyed in every part of the country. These cookie cutter symbols reflect the shapes of the season and decorations are limited only by children's imaginations.

Fruitcakes are perhaps the most universal holiday dessert, regardless of some personal opinions. Of course, gingerbread people and gingerbread houses not only test the creativity and patience of

113

bakers of every age but frequently produce some interesting results.

How about some almond crescents rolled in powdered sugar and at least one rum or bourbon ball? And, we can't forget those wonderful Christmas candies — all flavors of fudge, peanut brittle, marzipan and chocolates. As long as we have the ingredients, there's no limit to the possibilities. Will power will have to wait a couple of weeks — it's Christmas.

Most families in the United States finally sit down to their traditional Christmas dinner, consisting of turkey and dressing, mashed potatoes and gravy, cranberries, and of course, all those wonderful desserts. Some families add a special dish handed down from relatives, but often Christmas dinner is the same one that has been enjoyed for generations. We get out our best china, silver and linens, and bring candles and flowers to the table. Christmas dinner is a celebration — after all, it's Christ's birthday.

Mom probably has her own recipe for dressing, and, of course, Aunt Nancy wouldn't think of letting anyone else bring the pumpkin pie — her "secret recipe" is the only pumpkin pie this family eats on Christmas. And Grandma insists on making the gravy. It's all part of the wonderful traditions each family repeats with some variations year after year. Loved ones who come home for the holidays make sure they arrive for Christmas dinner — it's a time everyone is together.

What were the early Christmas feasts like? Did people celebrate the way we do today? What did they eat hundreds or even thousands of years ago?

One thing is certain, they ate a lot. In times past, holiday feasts were held in the winter after the herds were butchered and the crops harvested. These celebrations honored their gods and often lasted for days. Food was plentiful and there was time for revelry. In Rome, what began as a one-day festival of *Saturnalia,* eventually stretched from the middle of December to the new year. Persians held their winter solstice feast to honor Mithra, their deity of light. The pagan Teutonic tribes in northern Europe honored Woden by consuming great quantities of food and drink during the Yuletide Season. Some five thousand years ago, Egyptians held winter festivals where abundant food was an integral part of the celebration. Around the same time, the Mesopotamians held a new year's festival for twelve days to insure the return of their god of growing things, Tammuz. The Celts and Norsemen believed that the boar was a sacred animal, and the boar's head was a delicacy enjoyed at medieval banquets. Though most of the rituals in these celebrations revolved around honoring their gods, consuming lavish amounts of food seemed to enhance the festivities.

Myth has it that Christmas was first observed in England in 521 when King Arthur celebrated his victory over York with a feast at his famous round table. In the ninth century, Alfred the Great designated twelve days to food and festivities. After the Normans conquered England in 1066, Christmas became a time of prolonged feasting and gaiety until Twelfth Night, January 6. Medieval English kings celebrated Christmas with prodigious feasting. For example, in 1252 Henry III ordered six hundred fat oxen for the Christmas banquet. Not surprisingly, these bountiful feasts became very popular in England. Weeks of preparation went into the most important feast of the year which was Christmas. Members of royalty competed among themselves for the longest and most elaborate feast, with the spectacle starting at noon and lasting for nine or more hours.

An example of the outrageous size of these feasts is the following recipe for undoubtedly the most famous pie ever served at Christmas. It was made in England in 1770 for a party hosted by Sir Henry Grey. The pie was nine feet in circumference, weighed approximately 165 pounds, and had to be wheeled into the dining room on a cart. The recipe for this mincemeat pie, which was once called mutton pie and was often baked in the shape of a cradle, called for: four geese, two turkeys, four wild ducks, two rabbits, two curlews, seven blackbirds, six pigeons, four partridges, two bushels of flour, and twenty pounds of butter. This pie prompted the warning, "You dare not appear in Cornwall at Christmastime, or you might end up being baked in a pie."

The mincemeat pie contained rich and exotic spices which represented the treasures the Magi brought Jesus. It also contained fruits, especially apples, representing hope for a bountiful season.

In old England, the end of winter was often celebrated by killing and curing an ox. Not everyone could afford an ox, so many substituted pigs. Wild pigs or boars, were more plentiful than domestic ones, and hunting and killing wild boars was part of the appeal.

Ancient Druids revered the wild boar; they believed that when the boar dug his tusks into the ground, it introduced the practice of plowing the earth to plant crops. In pre-Christian days, as a sacrifice to the goddess Freya, Druids offered a boar's head at the winter solstice. The English adopted the custom, and it became a tradition at Christmas. King Henry VIII served a boar's head at his coronation feast. While the whole boar was roasted, the boar's head was served as the *pièce de résistance* at English holiday dinners. It was brought to the table with great ceremony by a procession of trumpeters and minstrels. Usually at those feasts the boar's head was served on a gold or silver platter, staring at guests with prune-filled eyes and a mouth stuffed with an orange.

Another popular dish in those days was the peacock. Cooks carefully removed the skin, keeping all the lavish feathers intact, then stuffed and seasoned the bird with spices and baked it. When it was partly cooled, the plumage, along with gilded beak and claws, were sewn back on. The colorful tail was spread out gracefully, and the lady of the house presented it to her guests on a silver platter.

Plum pudding was another favorite with the English. An old legend explains its origin:

A king and his men were lost in a blizzard while returning from a hunting trip on Christmas Eve. To prevent his men from starving, the king ordered his cook to concoct a dish from all the provisions that were left. This meant combining flour and potatoes with walnuts, fruit, chopped venison, brandy, sugar, spices and plums. All the ingredients were boiled in a bag and, since the cook had more plums than anything else, they called it plum pudding. Maybe the saving grace was that, before serving, brandy was poured over the top and the pudding was brought to the table flaming. Today's recipes usually substitute raisins for plums; although it is believed that raisins were actually called *plumbs* many years ago.

Some traditionalists believe plum pudding should be made months in advance so it can age properly. Many of the puddings made in the past were started several weeks before Christmas, partly because of a superstition. The pudding was made in a washtub, and everyone in the family, including young children, took a turn at stirring it. Children delighted in being asked to help, especially since, while stirring, they could make a secret wish which would surely come true in the new year. According to tradition, it was important to always stir clockwise to make a wish come true. Since the pudding was made of boiled wheat, milk, egg yolk, venison and mutton, the wishes probably were that the pudding would be edible. Each family had their own recipe, but the main idea was to "put good things in, and good things will come out." Each year, everyone tried to make this idea work by adding something new or different. One can imagine some of the results.

In 1603, King James I succeeded Queen Elizabeth I as ruler of England. James disliked the traditional boar's head and substituted wild turkey at his first Christmas dinner. He and his friends hunted the turkeys in the fields on his land. The turkey shoots served not only as fun sport but also provided a sumptuous meal.

The boar's head tradition never made the journey to the New World. Many of the new colonists arriving in the New England states weren't wealthy, and the lavish feasts enjoyed in England weren't copied in their new homes. However, wild turkeys were abundant in the new land, and though far from tender, their availability made the big birds a staple at Christmas dinner.

A traditional Christmas drink served in England was called "lambs wool," a mixture of hot ale, sugar, spices, beaten eggs, and roasted apples. Lambs wool was served from a large wassail bowl, with each guest exclaiming, *"Wes hal,"* meaning, "Good luck," or "To your health." Today we use a punch bowl to serve drinks at parties, and we still toast "To your health."

Though the traditional wassail bowl is no longer as popular as in Old England, another holiday drink has appeared at many Christmas gatherings. Eggnog, a combination of eggs, milk, sugar and spices, can be served hot or cold, with or without rum or bourbon. Eggnog appears to be an American invention, possibly a corruption of "egg 'n' grog," since grog was the name for rum in the colonies.

Perhaps the most elaborate Christmas feast and pageant held in the United States today is the Bracebridge Dinner at the Ahwahnee Hotel in Yosemite National Park. Based on Washington Irving's *Sketch Book,* it re-creates the Christmas festivities Irving experienced during his visits to English manors.

This authentic Christmas feast is a medieval pageant with the participants speaking in Old English, wearing Renaissance costumes. The three-hour dinner ceremony is announced by festive trumpeters. Each course is preceded by a representation of the actual dish. This consists of *papier mâché* replicas of a boar's head, fish, peacock, baron of beef, wassail bowl, and plum pudding. These dishes are presented to the squire, who makes a proclamation, then immediately serves each course. Minstrels and carolers entertain the guests throughout the dinner.

The Bracebridge dinner, started in 1927 when the hotel opened, has such worldwide appeal that they now have expanded it to five seatings — two on December 22 and 25, and one on December 24. Each seating accommodates 350 people. If you wish to attend, you must enter a lottery in January.

People in other countries eat special Christmas foods which are much different from a typical American menu. Pastries in some form are part of most everyone's Christmas feast, but the side dishes and entrees illustrate not only ethnic preferences but also regional products.

Some Italians fast twenty-four hours before Christmas Eve, then enjoy an elaborate banquet, which frequently includes a dish called *capitoni,* made from fried or steamed eels. A variety of pastas is usually included and special loaf-shaped Christmas bread called *panettone* is an Italian favorite.

Fish was an important symbol among early Christians, and in Scandinavian countries a Christmas Eve smorgasbord features *lutefisk,* a sun-dried cod served with cream sauce. A Christmas ham and vegetables, especially potatoes and cabbage, are followed by a special rice pudding which has an almond hidden inside. Tradition says that whoever finds the almond will marry in the next year. Roasted goose is often served for Christmas dinner in Norway, as are special buns decorated with frosting in the form of a cross to symbolize Christ. Christmas Eve in Norway is known as "dipping day" and each family member dips a piece of bread in a kettle filled with hot oil. When the bread is soaked through, participants give thanks and eat it as a reminder of those less fortunate. A popular Christmas meal in Finland is cold ham and pickled herring served with turnips, carrots and salted cucumbers. Gingerbread cookies, called *pepparkakor,* are made into shapes of animals, stars and houses. Finlanders enjoy *glogg,* a red wine simmered with raisins and spices with their Christmas dinner.

Roast goose is a traditional Christmas dish in some regions of France. An old legend says the goose cackled to welcome the Wise Men to the stable in Bethlehem. Other French regions serve ham and turkey, while oysters are popular in Paris. When the French return home from church on Christmas Eve, they enjoy a feast called *le reveillon*. It may feature as many as fifteen courses and often lasts until dawn. The highlight of the feast is a dense sponge cake shaped like a yule log with holly garnish.

In Alaska, many families eat caribou meat, fish pie and smoked salmon at their Christmas dinner. In Poland, after a day-long fast, as dusk settles and the first star appears on Christmas Eve, a feast begins by passing around a wafer called an *oplatek*. The *oplatek* has a picture of the Holy Family stamped on it. After each family member breaks off a piece, portions are given to the farm animals.

Austrians traditionally serve fish soup and carp, two loaves of bread representing the old and new testaments, and *lebkuchen,* heart-shaped cookies with Christmas sayings scrawled in frosting. In Greenland, *mattak,* whale skin with a slice of blubber inside, is passed around the dinner table. Though considered a delicacy, *mattak* is so tough to chew it is simply swallowed. Surprisingly, it tastes like fresh coconut. Auks are shorebirds indigenous to Greenland, and the Eskimos who live there consider the raw flesh of young auks a great delicacy. In preparation for Christmas dinner, auks are buried in sealskins for months, and served each year during the holiday season even though they are in an advanced stage of decomposition. Because Christmas comes in the middle of summer in Australia, cold turkey and salad are often served at a family picnic at the beach.

French-speaking Canadians follow the French tradition of the Christmas banquet, *le reveillon*. In British Columbia, smoked salmon sometimes accompanies the Christmas turkey.

People in Great Britain still enjoy plum pudding and mince pies. The boar's head has long since been replaced by turkey or prime rib with Yorkshire pudding. The first turkeys served in England were sent there by the colonists from North America in the 1600s. One of the few native American Christmas foods are cranberries. It is believed the Indians told the Pilgrims that the red berries growing in the bogs around Plymouth were good to eat, and that started the tradition of serving cranberries with turkey. America still exports cranberries to England.

Most Christmas traditions have common themes the world over, yet distinct differences are found in the menus for Christmas dinner. The common link across all cultures is that food is closely tied to their traditions, and is shared with neighbors, friends and loved ones. It's all part of what makes us different and yet the same, especially during that special time each year.

"It's The Holiday Season...."

XI

Santa Claus is Coming to Town

Santa Claus Is Coming To Town

Santa Claus

Saint Nicholas — Austria, Belgium, Greece

Svaty Nikulus — Czechoslovakia (Svatej Mikulas)

Santer Klausen — Austria

Sinterklaas — Holland

Father Christmas — England, Ireland, and other countries

Padre Nicholas — Brazil

Viejo Pascuero — Chile

Babbo Natale — Italy

The Three Kings — Spain, Mexico, Puerto Rico, Philippines

Julenisse — Scandinavia

Jultomten — Sweden

Julemanden — Denmark

Joulupukki — Finland

Julesvenn — Norway

Christkindle — Germany and Austria

Weihnachtsmann — Germany

Pelznickel — German

Babouschka — Russia

Le Befana — Italy

Hoteiosho — Japan

Lam Khoong-Khoong — China

Lad Ren — China

Père Noel — France

Babba Noel — Egypt

SANTA CLAUS!

You may not recognize all these names, but if you said *Hoteiosho* to a Japanese child, or *Le Befana* to an Italian child, their reaction would leave no doubt in your mind. This Christmas visitor may go by different names in different countries, but he creates the same magic each year in every child's heart. Once a year, this generous spirit becomes the most important person in the world to children. Little ones spend weeks carefully plotting what gifts they'll ask for, then write it all down in a letter to this mythical figure, along with their assurances that they have indeed been good. These same hopes were expressed by their parents and grandparents before them.

The questions don't change, either. In North America, where Santa Claus leaves gifts beneath the Christmas tree, children question as they have for hundreds of years: does he really, *really* know if I've been good or bad and, if so, how does he know? How does he slip down the chimney with that big, fat tummy? How does he manage to visit everyone's house in one night? How does he eat all those cookies and drink all that milk? What is it really like at the North Pole? How do reindeer fly? Did he get my letter?

There is only one answer to all the questions children have asked over the years: Santa Claus is *magic*!

Who is this magic person who goes by so many names? We have to travel back many years to learn how the myth of Santa Claus came about.

Nicholas was born in Patara in Asia Minor around 280 A.D. There are many legends surrounding him, but few known facts. He was orphaned at a young age and became a bishop in Myra, in Asia Minor. Nicholas was known for his kindness and generosity and for giving anonymous gifts at night. His good works inspired many people to join the Christian church. After his death around 343 A.D., people referred to him as a saint. The Eastern Catholic Church officially recognized his sainthood by 800 A.D. Because of the many legends about Nicholas' generous acts, he became known as the patron saint of sailors, marriageable maidens, bankers and thieves. But he was best known as the patron saint of children.

The name day of a saint is the day he or she dies. Nicholas died on December 6, and as he grew more popular, Saint Nicholas Eve, December 5, became an occasion for giving gifts in his honor. Several European countries still observe Saint Nicholas' Day, and children receive gifts in honor of the kindly saint.

After Nicholas' death, legends of his numerous good deeds spread, and hundreds of churches were built in his honor. Over time, his legend grew as the stories became more and more incredible. At some point he gained the power to fly and was depicted riding through the sky on a white horse, wearing the hat and red-and-white robes of a bishop and sporting a long, white beard.

Each year on Saint Nicholas Eve, it was believed that the saint traveled over the land, leaving gifts for good children and switches for the bad. In anticipation of his visit, children placed their shoes on the hearth, and left hay for Saint Nicholas' horse.

The pagan influence remained part of the myth of St. Nicholas, as he was usually accompanied by a small creature who took on many names and descriptions. This creature was almost always ugly and often sported horns. He had different and varied means of punishing naughty children, and carried rods, switches and sometimes even a whip to frighten them. He also had coal in a sack instead of presents. One of the best-known of these creatures was Black Peter (*Zwarte Piet*) who accompanied St. Nicholas in the Netherlands.

In the sixteenth century, saints lost their popularity in many parts of Europe. However, the custom of gift-exchanging, which dated back to pre-Christian days, was much too

popular to abandon. Those people who no longer believed in Saint Nicholas simply replaced him. The new patrons had different names, and many of them brought gifts on Christmas Eve instead of Saint Nicholas Eve.

The English assigned the role of bringing gifts to Father Christmas. He is a huge, bearded man in a red robe lined with fur who wears a crown of holly, ivy, or mistletoe and brings gifts on Christmas Eve. He often rides on a white donkey, or sometimes appears on a white goat.

In Spain, children believe the Three Wise Men bring gifts on the eve of Epiphany. They leave straw out for the Wise Men's camels, which is replaced by presents the next morning.

Padre Nicholas and his elf helpers arrive in Brazil in the middle of summer when children are on vacation. He slips into the houses through windows the children leave open and fills their shoes with gifts and treats.

Chinese children make stockings and "Nice Old Father" fills them with gifts. This bountiful spirit wears mandarin shoes and hat and carries lanterns. Chinese decorate with lanterns and other ornaments that light up, and compete for the biggest and most lavish display.

Italian children believe their presents come from *Befana,* an old woman who had been too busy to accompany the Wise Men to Bethlehem. In Russia, a different version of the story is told. *Baboushka* gave the Wise Men the wrong directions to Bethlehem and, like *Befana,* she still wanders the world each Epiphany Eve, leaving gifts for children, hoping one of them will be the Christ Child.

Swedish children receive their gifts on Christmas Eve from *Jultomten,* an elf who wears a red cap and has a long white beard. He, too, rides in a sleigh pulled by a goat. Before going to bed, Swedish children set out a bowl of porridge for *Jultomten,* and hay and carrots for his goat.

Scandinavian children believe their Christmas visitor has elves helping him make toys, who during the year spy on them to find out what they want for Christmas. The children also believe the gift-giver and his elves live in Lapland, a country with many, many reindeer to pull the sleighs.

Germans tell their children that the *Christkindl*, or Christ Child, brings them presents on Christmas Eve. They write letters asking for gifts, gluing the envelope and sprinkling it with sugar so it sparkles when left on the window sill, assuring the Christ Child will not miss it. The children believe the Holy Infant rides on a white donkey, so they leave straw out for the animal. The gifts brought by the *Christkindl* are called *Christ*

Christmas: Traditions and Legends

Bündles, which sometimes contain a birch rod tied to them to remind children to be good in the next year.

Holland continues to celebrate Saint Nicholas Day in December. Some say *Sinterklaas* arrives by boat from Spain, always accompanied by his servant, Black Peter. He wears bishop's red robes and rides a white horse. Black Peter carries a big sack filled with presents for good children, and birch rods for those who have been bad. On Christmas Eve in France, children leave their shoes in front of the fireplace for *Père Noel* to fill with presents. They believe he has been sent by Jesus. In Japan, an old priest, *Hoteiosho,* travels by foot and carries a backpack filled with presents. It is said he has eyes both in the front and back of his head. Children in Italy wait for *Befana,* who flies through the air on a broom. In Hawaii, Santa arrives by canoe, wearing a lei and sarong skirt.

When the Dutch came to America, their children continued the custom of leaving wooden shoes out for *Santa Niklaus* to fill. Over time, *Santa Niklaus* became *Sinter Klass* or *Sinter Claes,* which eventually became Santa Claus. Dutch children said *Sinter Klass* so fast it sounded like Santa Claus. Try it, and you'll see.

English immigrants who settled in New York and were not Puritans still celebrated Christmas and held onto their custom of waiting for Father Christmas to arrive on Christmas Eve. Eventually, the English and Dutch settlers who shared the land also merged their customs and celebrations.

An old myth in northern Europe tells about the god Thor riding through the sky in a chariot pulled by reindeer, though some reports suggest it was drawn by two white goats named Cracker and Gnasher. Over the years, Thor became Father Thor, then was called Father Christmas in early Germany. He was an old man with a long white beard who stopped at homes for holiday dinners and brought gifts for the children.

All these customs and legends contributed to the Santa Claus myth we still hold on to today. But there were also significant contributions made by Americans. In 1809, Washington Irving, writing under the name of Diedrich Knickerbocker, published a story about the Dutch in New York which included several references to Saint Nicholas as their patron saint. Instead of bishop's robes, he wore a wide-brimmed hat, smoked a pipe, and strongly resembled a "sturdy Dutchman." Irving claimed the saint rode over the tops of trees in a wagon, dropping gifts into chimneys.

Kwanzaa

Pancho Navidad

Hawaiian Santa

Doris Baines

Is there anyone among us who hasn't written Santa a letter explaining how good we've been and why we deserve to get a very special present this year? We all know Santa lives at the North Pole, so of course that is where we send our letter. What happens to requests from children who send a letter addressed just to Santa Claus, or to Santa Claus, North Pole? Or to Santa Claus, Indiana, or Christmas, Florida, or North Pole, New York? Well, Santa has a lot of helpers around the world who answer those letters. Many of them are senior citizens who have been helping Santa out for years. In Omaha, Nebraska, students in creative writing classes answer the letters. Most of the post offices, including the Santa Claus Main Post Office in Rovaniemi, Finland, which receives 500,000 letters annually, depend on volunteer elves to respond. Of course, they always pass on the requests to Santa. Like this one:

Dear Santa Claus,
 Momy says I have been gud this yer. Ples bring me a truk and some linkon logs. I will wach for you Christmas Eve and will leve carrots for your reinder. I love you.

Love,

Randy

 One thing that is certain is that Santa has to be able to decipher a four-, five-, or six-year old's spelling, which is in itself a challenge:
 "Dear Santa Clause,"
 "Dear Sana,"
 "Santa Claws"
 "some prety decorasons"
 "a thusne dollars for my mom"
 "some prtty rocks."
 "a matres for my bottom bed"

Christmas: Traditions and Legends

a new real Brother + sister

"a starrie-o"

"a new sister cause the old ones two meen"

Naturally children work very hard at convincing Santa they have been good, but some realize they would be a little less than truthful if they didn't temper this declaration:

"I have been god a lot of times"

"I've been a gud girl most of the time except for two days"

"I have been working on not hitting my sister"

I had been working on not hitting my Brother Heiden. Love Hari

"I have been good by giving my brother toys and letting him jump on me"

"Some days I am really berry good"

Children often include messages or inquiries about the reindeer, especially Rudolph:

"I will laeve cookes and carrtts for you and your raindeer"

"I like your reindeer, especially Rudolph and the girl he's going to marry"

"What stuff do you feed the reindeer to make them fly?"

"Tell Rudolph I love him"

"Don't let Rudolph catch cold on Christmas Eve"

A great variety of things are requested, some rather bizarre, some very poignant:

"...an elifant that blows out butterflies..."

"Please bring my sister new diapers"

"...most of all, I want you to bring my mommy some money, please"

Help pore people!

"...and a rabbit" (followed by "do not give him one, please" in different handwriting)

"I really, really want for Kyle to like me"

"I'm writing for my sister who is three years old. She would like a doll house, a Baby Bye-Bye, a fluffy puppy, a bulldozer and a truck"

"I want a stuff dog"

"I want a stuft aminal"

"A real puppy that will stay small"

At the beginning of a letter ... "$100" ... at the end of the letter ... "another $100 $"

"You know what's on my list — as always — I'm not telling anyone else"

Others just ask questions or leave special messages:

"I'm six years old — how old are you?"

"And, please put the presents under the tree this year"

"I will leave you diet coke and cookies"

"I will leave you a pese of my Halowen candy"

"Plees right back"

"Please leave a mesage"

"Call me if you get bored"

"Go to my house first"

"I would like to stay up and meet you but I'm always too tired.

Although children send letters to Santa at the North Pole, some of them will still take their wish list along when visiting Santa. The list will either be crumpled up in the child's fist and barely readable, or so perfectly preserved it appears to have never been touched by little hands. Children look forward to their visit with Santa

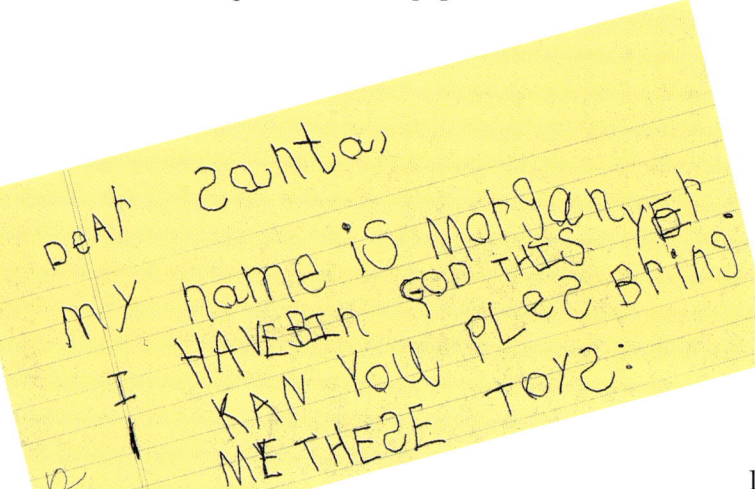

for weeks, changing their minds many times on what to say to the jolly man with the white beard in the red suit. A small child's first encounter with a real, live Santa Claus can be overwhelming and often results in loud and healthy screams for "Mommy!"

The following year that same child most probably will jump up into Santa's lap, giving him a big hug and a kiss. Looking at old pictures of our children's visits to Santa creates a mixture of emotions which stir up wonderful memories.

These pictures are proudly displayed each year, and become part of the decorations we cherish during the Christmas season.

Santa reports reveal some interesting conversations. One young Santa visitor eagerly informed him he knew how to get to the North Pole. When Santa asked for directions, the child replied, "You start at Texas, then go through Arizona, and you're there!"

Another youngster asked for a rather unusual gift. "Santa, could you please bring me some oat bran?" Best of all, one child expressed that which makes every Santa Claus proud and pleased to be sharing the dreams and hopes of children everywhere, "Santa, I love you, and I will always believe in you!"

The Image of Santa

Clement C. Moore was a professor of divinity at New York Theological Seminary. He was also the father of six small children, and he liked to write verse. He read and enjoyed Irving's book and in 1822 decided to write a Christmas poem for his children. The poem centered around Saint Nicholas, whom he portrayed as "chubby and plump, a right jolly old elf." Some of the poem seems to come directly from Irving's book: "…and laying his finger aside of his nose," while other parts of it were apparently borrowed from an anonymous poem published a year before Moore wrote his version. In this poem, "Old Santeclaus" rides in a sleigh pulled by one reindeer, "O'er chimney-tops and tracks of snow / To bring his yearly gifts to you." As we all know, one reindeer became "eight tiny reindeer" with names we all memorize as children. This poem, *A Visit From Saint Nicholas,* better known today as *The Night Before Christmas,* has become one of our most popular Christmas classics and, though it clearly describes him, there is no mention of Santa Claus.

From this description in Moore's poem, artists began to create images of the jolly Christmas visitor. In 1863, *Harper's Weekly* published the first pen-and-ink Santa Claus illustration by Thomas Nast, who illustrated a Santa annually for *Harper's Weekly* for the next twenty-three years. He remembered Moore's poem from his childhood and clearly called on that memory for his Santa.

"He was dressed all in red, from his head to his toe, / And the beard on his chin was as white as the snow. … He had a broad face and a little round belly," are all quotes from Moore's poem, which perfectly describe the Santa drawn by Nast. He also drew Santa in his workshop at the North Pole, making toys and checking lists to "find out who's naughty and nice." In 1882, he was the first to declare that Santa lived at the North Pole, causing a great scramble between British and Scandinavian explorers to discover his workshop. Nast also included in his drawings elves helping Santa. Thus, the beloved but thin bishop who became Saint Nicholas was replaced by the beloved but plump and jolly Santa Claus.

Another memorable image of Santa Claus was created in 1931 for the Coca-Cola Company. The company hired Haddon Sundholm to create an advertising campaign linking their product to the good feelings associated with the holiday season. The Santa that Sundholm painted was similar to the one described in Moore's poem, but he was huge. His suit was fur-trimmed, he wore black leather boots and a large black leather belt around his ample tummy, and boasted a long white beard and a cheery, happy face. The Coca-Cola campaign lasted from 1931 to 1966 and appeared in magazines, posters, and larger-than-life billboards. Santa Claus had surely come to town.

A Visit From Saint Nicholas

by Clement C. Moore

'Twas the night before Christmas, when all through the house
Not a creature was stirring, not even a mouse;
The stockings were hung by the chimney with care,
In hopes that Saint Nicholas soon would be there.

The children were nestled all snug in their beds,
While visions of sugar-plums danced in their heads;
And Mama in her kerchief and I in my cap,
Had just settled our brains for a long winter's nap.

When out on the lawn there arose such a clatter,
I sprang from the bed to see what was the matter;
Away to the window I flew like a flash,
Tore open the shutters and threw up the sash.

The moon on the breast of the new-fallen snow
Gave the lustre of midday to objects below;
When, what to my wondering eyes should appear,
But a miniature sleigh and eight tiny reindeer.

With a little old driver, so lively and quick,
I knew in a moment it must be Saint Nick.
More rapid than eagles his coursers they came,
And he whistled, and shouted, and called them by name:

"Now, Dasher!Now, Dancer! Now, Prancer and Vixen.!
On, Comet! On Cupid! On, Donder and Blitzen!
To the top of the porch! To the top of the wall!
Now, dash away! Dash away! Dash away all!"

As dry leaves that before the wild hurricane fly,
When they meet with an obstacle, mount to the sky,
So up to the house-top the coursers they flew,
With a sleigh full of toys — and Saint Nicholas too.

And then in a twinkling, I heard on the roof,
The prancing and pawing of each little hoof.
As I drew in my head, and was turning around,
Down the chimney Saint Nicholas came with a bound.

He was dressed all in fur, from his head to his foot,
And his clothes were all tarnished with ashes and soot;
A bundle of toys he had flung on his back,
And he looked like a peddler just opening his pack.
His eyes — how they twinkled! His dimples, how merry!
His cheeks were like roses, his nose like a cherry!
His droll little mouth was drawn up like a bow,
And the beard on his chin was as white as the snow.

The stump of a pipe he held tight in his teeth,
And the smoke it encircled his head like a wreath.
He had a broad face, and a little round belly,
That shook when he laughed, like a bowl-full of jelly.

He was chubby and plump, a right jolly old elf,
And I laughed when I saw him, in spite of myself.
A wink of his eye and a twist of his head,
Soon gave me to know I had nothing to dread.

He spoke not a word, but went straight to his work,
And filled all the stockings; then turned with a jerk,
And, laying his finger aside of his nose,
And giving a nod, up the chimney he rose.

He sprang to his sleigh, to his team gave a whistle,
And away they all flew, like the down of a thistle.
But I heard him exclaim, ere he drove out of sight,
"Happy Christmas to all!
And to all a good night!"

Hanging Stockings

Santa's most important chore is to fill our stockings on Christmas Eve. Remember in the poem: "The stockings were hung by the chimney with care, In hopes that Saint Nicholas soon would be there…" Many of us have our own stocking with our name stitched on it. It may be our given name, or say "Mom," "Dad," "Grandma," or "Grandpa." Christmas stockings hanging on the mantel, filled with special treats, are a welcome and exciting sight to a child on Christmas morning. This story of the Christmas stocking explains where this custom came from:

Saint Nicholas loved to bestow gifts but never wanted anyone, especially children, to know where the presents came from. Frequently he left his gifts at night, when he was sure no one would see him. Nicholas had heard of a poor man in a village whose wife had died and left him with three unmarried daughters. The man had little money for food or clothes for his daughters and no money for their dowries so they could get married. In those days, if a girl did not have a dowry, she had little chance of getting a husband.

Finally, the father, who was desperate, decided the only solution to his problem was to sell his three daughters into slavery. He called them all together to explain his terrible decision. They were young and beautiful girls who were close to each other and devoted to their father. They missed their mother, but felt if the family could stay together, everything would be all right.

"You asked us to meet with you this morning, Father," the oldest girl said. "Is anything wrong?"

"We know you are very sad, and that you miss our mother very much," the middle daughter told her father. "But, we must stay together until we can find a suitable husband to take care of us."

The youngest daughter put her arms around her father and squeezed him. "You are a wonderful father, and we all love you very much. We know how hard you work to try to keep us fed and clothed, and we promise to try to help more."

The father couldn't tell them what he had decided to do. He must find some other way to keep his family together until his daughters married.

Saint Nicholas was traveling through their town and overheard some of the villagers talking about the man's troubles. He stayed in the village overnight, and the next morning, when the man and his daughters came into the kitchen, the oldest girl's stocking, which had been hung by the fireplace to dry, had a lump of gold in it. No one could imagine where it had come from, but the oldest daughter now had a dowry and could get married. A few months later, a lump of gold appeared in the middle daughter's stocking, and a few months after that the youngest daughter, too, found a lump of gold in her stocking. Word spread about the good fortune of the sisters, and soon people from all over were hanging their stockings by the chimney to dry, in hopes that they, too, would wake up and find a treasure in them. No one knew it was Saint Nicholas who climbed up on the roof and threw the lumps of gold down the chimney, where they landed in the stockings. However the custom of hanging stockings to be filled with treasures is still observed hundreds of years later.

Some believe Santa puts an apple in the toe of your stocking and an orange in the heel if you have been good. Others think the orange symbolizes the lump of gold from Saint Nicholas. How about a nut just for fun, some salt for good luck, and a piece of coal to keep you warm? Children in Italy put wooden shoes out for *Le Befana,* and they believe she fills the shoes of good children with toys and sweets, while bad children find rocks or ashes in their shoes. A lump of coal is sometimes believed to indicate bad behavior in America.

What name children give the Christmas Eve visitor is not important. Who fills their stocking or shoe with presents doesn't matter. Children all over the world will continue to look forward to that one special night. Every year children look in wonderment at the Santas, the Kris Kringles, the Saint Nicholases around them and wonder if they have really been good enough to have their wishes come true.

And even when a child reaches the age when the truth about Santa must be told, the experience of believing in Santa Claus, if only for a short time, is a magical part of growing up. And perhaps the best truth of all is that Santa keeps us all from ever *really* growing up.

"The one real Santa Claus is the one in your heart."

Yes, Virginia, There Is A Santa Claus

Perhaps the most famous letter ever sent at Christmas was not to sent to Santa but was written about him. It first appeared on the editorial page of the New York *Sun* on September 21, 1897. The letter, from an eight-year-old girl, was answered by Frank Church, the editor:

Dear Editor,
I am eight years old. Some of my little friends say there is no Santa Claus. Papa says, "If you see it in the *Sun* it's so." Please tell me the truth, is there a Santa Claus?

Virginia O'Hanlon
115 West 95th Street
New York City

"Virginia, your little friends are wrong. They have been affected by the skepticism of a skeptical age. They do not believe except what they see. They think that nothing can be which is not comprehensible by their little minds. All minds, Virginia, whether they be men's or children's, are little. In this great universe of ours man is a mere insect, an ant, in his intellect, as compared with the boundless world about him, as measured by the intelligence capable of grasping the whole of truth and knowledge.

Yes, Virginia, there is a Santa Claus. He exists as certainly as love and generosity and devotion exist, and you know that they abound and give to your life its highest beauty and joy. Alas! how dreary would be the world if there were no Santa Claus! It would be as dreary as if there were no Virginias. There would be no childlike faith then, no poetry, no romance to make tolerable this existence. We should have no enjoyment, except in sense and sight. The eternal light with which childhood fills the world would be extinguished.

Not believe in Santa Claus! You might as well not believe in fairies! You might get your papa to hire men to watch in all the chimneys on Christmas Eve to catch Santa Claus, but even if they did not see Santa Claus coming down, what would that prove? Nobody sees Santa Claus, but that is no sign there is no Santa Claus. The most real things in the world are those that neither children nor men can see. Did you ever see fairies dancing on the lawn? Of course not, but that's no proof that they are not there. Nobody can conceive or imagine all the wonders there are unseen and unseeable in the world.

You tear apart a baby's rattle and see what makes the noise inside, but there is a veil covering the unseen world which not the strongest man, nor even the united strength of all the strongest men that ever lived, could tear apart. Only faith, fancy, poetry, love, romance, can push aside that curtain and view and picture the supernal beauty and glory beyond. Is it all real? Ah, Virginia, in all this world there is nothing else real and abiding.

No Santa Claus! Thank God he lives, and he lives forever. A thousand years from now, Virginia, nay ten thousand years from now, he will continue to make glad the heart of childhood."

The Legend Of Befana The Ageless Wanderer

Befana was an elderly woman who lived in a lonely cottage on the edge of a small village in Italy. Since she was not very friendly, the children in the village did not like her and they called her a "cranky old lady," and they were right. "All she ever does is clean her house," they complained, and they were right. Befana was too busy to care. All she really cared about was that her little cottage was spotless.

Every day Befana swept. She swept her house, she swept her front steps, and she swept the walkway; she didn't even know how many brooms she had worn out because she swept each morning *and* each afternoon. When Befana wasn't sweeping, she was baking or dusting or scouring or shining. Befana was always busy.

Befana lived near a great highway on which caravans frequently travelled. Even though Befana did not speak to the people who passed by her home, she had heard rumors in the village of a Child to be born; a Child that would rule the world in a kind and wonderful way. The villagers also talked about a star in the sky, the biggest and brightest star ever seen that would lead the Magi to the Child King. The villagers were out every night, excitedly scanning the evening sky for the star.

"Such a lot of fussing over a star." Befana muttered. "The sky is full of stars every night. What can be so special about this one?" And she went back to her cleaning.

One morning she got up at daybreak as usual. She had such a busy day ahead, sweeping and cleaning and baking. She had barely wrapped her hands around the broom to get started when she heard a loud knocking on her door. Befana sighed impatiently. "Now what?" she demanded. When Befana opened the door, she jumped in astonishment. Standing before her were three men, dressed like grand kings, wearing beautiful robes and magnificent crowns. One had a long beard white as snow, one was young, and the third was dark-skinned. Their arms were full of lovely gifts — boxes of jewels and sweet-smelling oils and ointments.

"We have come from far away," they told Befana, "and we are here to tell you of the birth of the Baby Jesus in Bethlehem. We are taking the Christ Child these gifts, for He was born to rule the world and teach all men to be loving and kind. The bright star in the heavens has guided us and will lead us to this King. Come with us, Befana. We will take you to the Christ Child, and you can look upon His face as He receives our gifts."

"Oh," Befana thought, "how I would love to go with them." However, she was frightened to leave her home, and besides, she had no lovely gifts to give to the Baby Jesus. *Most of all,* she hadn't even started her cleaning for the day. She wanted to explain all of this to the Wise Men, but she couldn't, so she simply shook her head.

"We are sad you will not come with us," one of the kings told Befana. "Indeed, you will be sorry if you stay at home and do not visit the Son of God. Word has spread throughout the countryside about the Baby Jesus being born in a manger in Bethlehem. Please change your mind."

Befana did not know what to do. She longed to go, but it had been such a long time since she had left her village, and she couldn't just leave right now. She needed to pack and she wanted to finish her housework and she needed to have a gift — it was just too much. "I'll follow you tomorrow," she told them. "I will have time to get ready and to find a present for the Baby Jesus. I will hurry so I can catch up with you and join you for the rest of the journey."

Befana watched the Wise Men leave. She closed the door to her cottage, then spent the day finishing her chores, but her mind kept going back to their invitation. She was glad she had decided to follow them, but now she must find a gift. Befana slowly walked over to an old chest in the corner. She had not opened it for a very long time, as there were many painful memories inside that chest. Slowly, she reached in and pulled out a straw doll. Tears began to stream down her face as she caressed it and remembered her dead baby. The thought of parting with the doll made her sad. It was dressed in a garment she had made from her wedding dress. Then her eyes found a large seed her child had used as a ball. Should she take these to the Christ Child? The gifts the Wise Men had were so much grander. But she remembered they had told her Jesus had been born in a manger of poor parents. She imagined Him playing with the toys her precious child had loved and wrapped them in a piece of cloth and put them in a basket.

By this time it was getting late, but Befana was too excited to sleep. She decided she could not wait until morning. If she left now, she would have a much better chance of catching up with the Wise Men, so she blew out her candle, locked her door and left, clutching the basket under her arms.

Befana stood in front of her cottage and realized she had no idea how far Bethlehem was, or even which way it was. All she could remember was that the Wise Men had disappeared over the hill. She started walking, deciding that when morning came, she could ask for help in finding her way.

"Can you show me the way to Bethlehem?" she asked everyone she met. But no one knew. Befana wandered that day and the next and the next, up and down roads, hurrying through fields and woods and towns, asking everybody, "Do you know the way to Bethlehem? I have gifts for the Christ Child, and I have lost my way." No one could tell her — all they answered was, "You must go farther, Befana. You must go farther." The bright star that had guided the Wise Men was gone, and she knew she had waited too long to follow them. Befana never caught up with the Wise Men, and she never found Bethlehem or the Baby Jesus.

Legend says that in Italy Befana is still looking for the Christ Child. Each Epiphany Eve, when the children are sound asleep, Befana walks softly through the villages, wrapped in a long cloak and carrying a bundle of toys. She quietly goes into the children's bedrooms and shines a candle in each child's face. "Is this the Christ Child?" she asks hopefully. "Is the Christ Child here?" Then she turns away sadly, saying, "I must go farther." Before she leaves, she places a toy on the pillow of each child "for His sake" and hurries on in her search for the Baby Jesus.

Doris Baines

Baboushka: A Russian Legend

Baboushka sits before the fire
Upon a winter's night;
The driving winds heap up the snow,
Her hut is snug and tight;
The howling winds — they only make
Baboushka's more bright.

She hears a knocking at the door
So late — who can it be?
She hastes to lift the wooden latch,
No thought of fear has she;
The wind-blown candle in her hand
Shines out on strangers three.

Their beards are white with age, and snow
That in the darkness flies;
Their floating locks are long and white,
But kindly are their eyes
That sparkle underneath their brows,
Like stars in frosty skies.

"Baboushka, we have come from far,
We tarry but to say,
A little Prince is born this night,
Who all the world shall sway.
Come join the search; come, go with us,
Who go our gifts to pay."

Baboushka shivers at the door:
"I would I might behold
The little Prince who shall be King,
But, ah! the night is cold,
The wind so fierce, the snow so deep,
And I, good sirs, am old."

The strangers three, no word they speak,
But fade in snowy space.
Baboushka sits before her fire,
And dreams, with wistful face:
"I would that I had questioned them,
So I the way might trace.

"When morning comes with blessed light,
I'll early be awake;
My staff in hand I'll go — perchance,
Those strangers I'll o'ertake;
And, for the Child some little toys
I'll carry, for His sake."

The morning came, and, staff in hand,
She wandered in the snow.
She asked the way of all she met,
But none the way could show.
"It must be farther yet," she sighed
"Then farther will I go."

And still, 'tis said, on Christmas Eve,
When high the drifts are piled,
With staff, with basket on her arm,
Baboushka seeks the child:
At every door her face is seen —
Her wistful face and mild.

Her gifts at every door she leaves;
She bends, and murmurs low,
Above each little face half-hid
By pillows white as snow:
"And, is He here?" Then softly sighs,
"Nay, farther must I go."
– Edith Matilda Thomas
– From Children of Christmas,
by Edith M. Thomas

XIII

Happy Holidays!

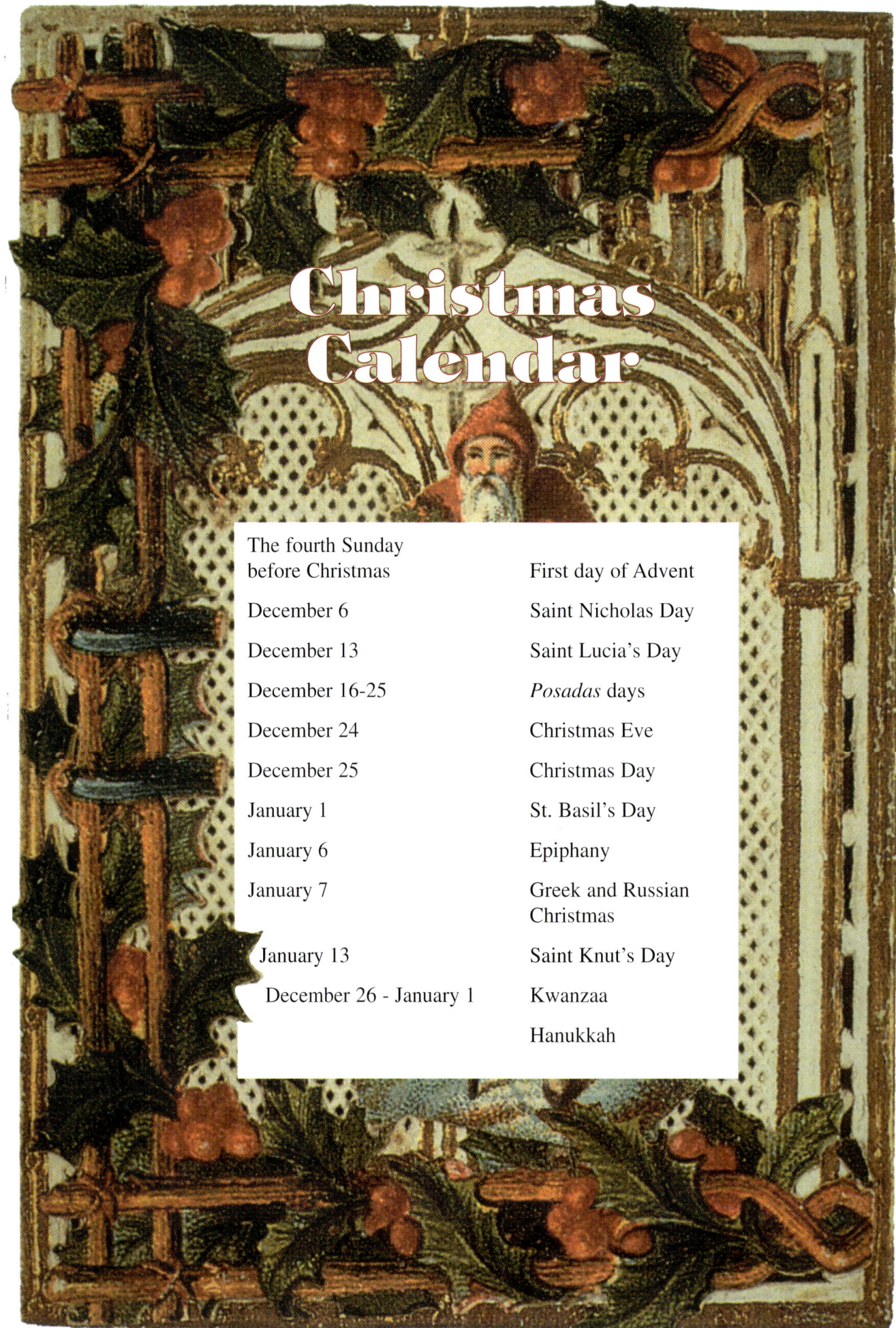

Christmas Calendar

The fourth Sunday before Christmas	First day of Advent
December 6	Saint Nicholas Day
December 13	Saint Lucia's Day
December 16-25	*Posadas* days
December 24	Christmas Eve
December 25	Christmas Day
January 1	St. Basil's Day
January 6	Epiphany
January 7	Greek and Russian Christmas
January 13	Saint Knut's Day
December 26 - January 1	Kwanzaa
	Hanukkah

Advent Calendars

The word "advent" is from the Latin term meaning "coming," and to Christians throughout the world, it is a time to contemplate the coming of Christ. Advent starts at the beginning of December and ends Christmas Day. The four Sundays before Christmas are known as Advent Sundays, and for many Christians they are a time for prayer and meditation, awaiting the celebration of the birth of Christ.

Other countries have somewhat different calendars and special days to celebrate. In Mexico, people celebrate the nine days prior to Christmas in processions called *posadas,* which means "inn" or "lodging." Homes are decorated by December 16, and the children, carrying figures representing Joseph and Mary, visit neighbors and friends, singing and asking for shelter for the Holy Family. Sometimes, adults play the parts of Joseph and Mary. In these dramas the callers are always turned away. The manger for the Baby Jesus remains empty until Christmas Eve, when a doll is added. Christmas in Mexico ends with observance of Epiphany on January 6.

In the Scandinavian countries, especially Sweden, Christmas observance begins December 13, Saint Lucia's Day. Swedish and German people have two Christmas days, one on December 25 and another December 26. The first is a traditional family and religious day, and the second is a day of partying and visiting friends, with emphasis on lots of food. Saint Knut's Day, January 13, ends the festive season. The day honors King Knut IV, who ruled from 1080 to 1086 and declared that Christmas should be celebrated for twenty days.

Three weeks constitute the Christmas season in Italy, starting eight days before Christmas and ending January 6. Small gifts may be exchanged Christmas Eve, but Befana brings most of the presents on the Twelfth Night.

December 6, Saint Nicholas Day, opens the Christmas season in several countries, including France, Belgium, Austria and Holland. The Greek and Russian Orthodox Christmas is celebrated on January 7 which, according to the Gregorian calendar, is the same as December 25.

In Germany, children begin preparing for Christmas on December 1 by opening the windows of an advent calendar. This has become a popular custom in America as well. It's always exciting to anticipate a birthday, and you can count the days until Christ's birthday with twenty-four numbered windows to open. Behind each "window" is a Christmas picture, of which the last one is the nativity scene, symbolizing the birth of Christ. The opening of these windows each day is said to represent the opening of your heart's window for Jesus to enter it at Christmastime. Originally the calendars were advent houses, with an appropriate Bible verse behind each door.

Another version of the advent calendar is a wreath on which twenty-four wrapped boxes are hung. Each box is numbered on the outside and contains a tiny present. In recent years, some rather elaborate and expensive versions of the advent calendar have become available. One is a wooden box with twenty-four separate compartments, each holding a tiny Christmas ornament. On top of the box is a large Christmas tree and Santa Claus cutout. As you remove the toys from the boxes, you hang them on the tree. It is a lovely way to enjoy the age-old custom of daily anticipating the holiday season

Doris Baines

Merry Christmas in Different Languages

Merry Christmas	United States, Great Britain, Australia, Canada
Froohliche Weihnachten	Germany
Joyeux Noel	France
Gledelig Jul	Norway
Glaedelig Jul	Denmark
Efithismena Kerstroeten	Netherlands
Happy Christmas	England
Hauskaa Joulua	Finland
Gud Jul	Sweden
Buon Natale	Italy
Felices Pascuas	Spain, Mexico
Hristos Razdajetsja	Russia, Alaska (Hriztos Razdaetsya)
Happy Hanukkah/Shalom	Israel
Feliz Navidad	Mexico, Guatemala
Mele Kalikimaka	Hawaii
Maligayang Pasko	The Philippines
Kala Christougena	Greece
Melkm Ganna	Ethiopia
Shen Dan Jieh	China (Holy Birth Festival)
Nadolig Llawen	Wales
Boas Festas	Portugal
Vroolik Kerfeest	The Netherlands

Christmas Cards

One of our warmest Christmas traditions came from England less than two hundred years ago. This tradition has nothing to do with fire, the sun, or any of the other many superstitions. It has everything to do with warmth, friendship and love.

Each year we anxiously await the beginning of the Christmas season, hoping we will hear from loved ones. Were it not for the Christmas season, we would probably lose contact with many former classmates, old friends and distant relatives. We may put off corresponding all year, but when the holiday season approaches, we look forward to our annual exchange of greetings. We announce news of births, family happenings, travel experiences, career plans and accomplishments,

and memories of times spent together. We even share the sad times we all encounter. When snapshots are included, we watch children grow into teenagers, then become adults with their own families. It is such a wonderful way to stay in touch with old friends.

There has long been a dispute in England over who created the first Christmas card. Sir Henry Cole, a London museum director, is generally awarded that distinction. As a child, he and his friends made "Christmas Pieces," which they gave to their parents and teachers to demonstrate their improving writing skills. Some of these pieces contained bible characters or scenes, others had printed borders with drawings of birds or flowers. It is believed many of them also contained strong hints for Christmas gifts.

In 1843, Sir Henry hired an artist friend, John

145

Horsley, to design a picture card with a Christmas greeting, after deciding it would be easier to send pre-made cards than to labor over individual greetings for his friends.

Sir Henry strongly believed in helping the needy, so he had the card designed to portray "feeding the hungry" and "clothing the naked." The card consisted of three panels, hinged so that the two side panels could be folded over the center one. The two outer panels depict the poor being clothed and fed, while the center one displays a festive gathering of family and friends, some of whom were celebrating the holiday by consuming wine. The card created quite a furor among Puritans in England, who declared it promoted drunkenness.

Sir Henry had one thousand of the cards printed. Those he did not use himself he sold for one shilling each. They all sold. The message on the card read: "A Merry Christmas and a Happy

New Year to You."

At first, only the wealthy could afford this delightful new custom of sending cards. Color printing was prohibitive, and artists were hired to design the greetings. The royal family solicited famous artists to paint their cards, which they had reproduced. The popularity of greeting cards spread, however, and less-expensive color printing soon became available. An improved postal system encouraged more participation, and by the end of the 1850s, Christmas greetings were well established as a tradition in England.

Christmas cards did not become popular in America until the mid-1870s. Louis Prang, a German immigrant, designed and printed such beautiful colored pictures on his cards that he became known as the "father of American Christmas cards." By 1881, he was printing five million cards a year and offering considerable cash prizes to artists to create Christmas card designs. In one year alone, more than six hundred artists competed for a total of $3,000 in award monies.

As popular as Prang's cards were, they were impractical to produce. By the end of the nineteenth century, less expensive cards flooded the market, forcing Prang out of business. Prior to World War I, many of the cards sold in America came from Germany. After the war, America got into the greeting card business.

Over the years, Christmas cards have reflected the times. Wars, fashions, fads, even science and technology affect the trends in Christmas greetings. Humorous cards often tackle these subjects, some displaying better taste than others; upon receiving a fruitcake, the punch line is, "Nobody wants to get food that will outlive them." Or, "Christmas is just plain weird. What other time of the year do you sit in front of a dead tree eating candy out of your socks?"

There are over two-and-a-half billion Christmas cards exchanged each year. You can find a card for anyone and for anyone's taste. Want to send a card from your cat to your neighbor's cat? Do you want to send a card to your boss, your teacher, your children or grandchildren, your butcher, your baker? They're all there. There are big cards, little cards, fancy and plain cards, cards that play tunes, and cards that contain snacks.

With all these choices, the Christmas card which remains a favorite with most people has a religious theme. The familiar nativity scene, Madonna and Child, stars and angels, the Three Wise Men, peace on earth — all these symbols remind us of the true significance of Christmas. We send our love through the message in the Christmas card we give, but we send it in remembrance of the birth of the Christ Child on that first Christmas Eve in Bethlehem.

Christmas Seals

The Christmas Seal® originated in Denmark in 1904. Einar Holboell, a young postal clerk, was concerned about the needy children afflicted with tuberculosis. Noticing the tremendous increase in mail during the Christmas season, he devised a plan to print and sell special Christmas Seals for letters and packages. It was his hope that the Christmas spirit would persuade people to buy them if they knew the money would help those sick children.

In 1904, the first year, more than four million seals were sold for a half-penny apiece, raising $18,000, which provided enough to build two children's TB hospitals.

In 1907, Christmas Seals were introduced in America by Miss Emily Bissell, an active supporter of the American Red Cross. Tuberculosis was the leading cause of death in the United States at that time. Miss Bissell's cousin, a doctor in a hospital which treated tuberculosis patients, asked her to help raise funds for the hospital. She had read about the success of the Christmas Seals in Denmark, and thought it would be a wonderful way to solve her cousin's problem.

Miss Bissell designed a seal with a red cross in the center and a half-wreath of holly above the words, "Merry Christmas." Fifty thousand were printed, and the first seals were sold in the Wilmington, Delaware, post office on December 7, 1907.

Miss Bissell's enthusiasm about the seals was not shared by the public, and she quickly realized she would have to take drastic measures to raise the $300 needed by her cousin. She took her cause to Philadelphia's leading newspaper, and the editor-in-chief was persuaded to support the campaign. That year $3,000 was raised, and $135,000 the following year.

The Red Cross sponsored the Christmas Seal until 1919. It was joined by the National Association for the Study and Prevention of Tuberculosis in 1910. That association, which is now the American Lung Association, eventually took over the Christmas Seal Campaign®. The red double-barred cross became their emblem.

Since 1908, famous artists have been asked to design each year's Christmas Seal. In 1975, schoolchildren in all fifty states, Washington, D.C., Guam, Puerto Rico, and the Virgin Islands, submitted designs. One from each state and territory was chosen, and a sheet of 1975 Christmas Seals contained fifty-four different designs. This practice was continued through 1980.

Christmas Seals today allow the American Lung Association to fight lung disease through education, community service, advocacy and research. In 1997, the 90th Anniversary of the Christmas Seal, the American Lung Association established the Emily Bissell Lung Health Award to be given to a female volunteer for her contribution to better health in her community..

Over forty countries now participate in Einar Holbell's Christmas Seal concept. Before his death in 1927, he had been decorated and knighted by several monarchs. Emily Bissell was a tireless worker for the campaign into the 1940s. She appeared with presidents, celebrities and other public figures, whom she convinced to support her cause.

First Christmas Seal of the American Lung Association, December 1907

The Little Match Girl

Translated from Hans Christian Andersen

It was bitterly cold that last evening of the old year. The snow was falling and darkness was closing in. A small girl, barely visible in the dim light, was wandering aimlessly through the streets, her head and feet both bare. She was wearing slippers when she left home, but they had belonged to her mother so were too big for the little girl. Earlier in the day, when scurrying across the street to avoid two carriages that were speeding by much too fast, she lost one of the slippers completely. A young boy grabbed the other one and ran down the street yelling that he would use it as a cradle when he had children.

The little girl walked on with her naked feet, blue and swollen from the cold. She carried some matches in her hand, and her apron pocket held more. No one had bought a match all day so she had not earned even a penny. Shaking from cold and hunger, she dragged through the streets, a sorrowful sight. Poor child. Snowflakes fell on her long yellow hair, but she paid no attention.

Lights shone from every window she passed and the delicious smell of roast goose floated through the air. Now she remembered it was New Year's Eve, but she decided not to think about that.

As night fell, she found a spot between two houses, sank down and huddled in a corner. She tried to warm her freezing feet by tucking them underneath her but they got even colder. She couldn't go home because she hadn't sold any matches and was afraid her father would beat her. Besides, it wasn't much warmer at home. The wind howled through the roof of her home even though they had stuffed the holes with straw and old rags.

By now her tiny hands were numb from the cold. If she could only strike a match to warm them. She held one, struck it against the brick wall of her house, and felt the warmth on her hands. The bright light was like a little candle. It felt so wonderful on her freezing hands, it seemed like she was sitting by a huge iron stove trimmed in brass. The fire made her hands feel so warm the little girl stretched out her feet to warm them. At that moment, the flame on the match flickered out, the image of the stove disappeared, and she was left alone with half a burned match in her hand.

She struck another match against the wall and its flame was so bright she could see inside the house. A snowy white tablecloth covered the table, which was set with the most beautiful dishes and silverware the little girl had ever seen. In the center of the table was a roast goose stuffed with apples and prunes. Then, to the girl's amazement, the goose jumped down from the platter and waddled across the floor towards her, with a knife and fork stuck in his breast. She held out her arms toward the goose, but then again the match went out, leaving her alone leaning against the cold dark wall.

She lit a third match and this time she was sitting under a Christmas tree even more beautiful than the one she had seen through the door of the rich merchants. Thousands of tapers glowed on the tree branches and lovely colored pictures looked down at her. The little girl stretched out her hand to touch the tapers, but once again the match burned out. The candles seemed to rise towards the sky, higher and higher until they became the stars. One of the stars fell, leaving a bright streak behind. "Someone is dying," the little girl thought. Her old grandmother, who was dead, and who was the only living soul who had ever loved her, had once told her that a falling star meant a soul was going to God.

She rubbed another match against the wall, and in the light of the flame, she clearly saw her grandmother standing in front of her, a kind and loving smile on her face. "Oh Grandmother," she cried, "please take me with you. I know you, too, will disappear when the match burns out, just like the stove and the goose and the tree." The little girl hurriedly lit all the matches she had left in her bundle, so she could keep her grandmother there with her. The bundle burned so brightly the night turned as light as day. Her grandmother had never been more beautiful. She swept the little girl in her arms and both flew upward to where there would be neither cold nor hunger nor suffering; to be with God.

At dawn the next morning, the little child still lay in her corner with rosy cheeks and a sweet smile. She had frozen to death. The first sun of the new year shone down on the frozen corpse still holding the burned out matches in her little hands. Some said she had tried to keep warm, but none imagined the beautiful sights she had seen or the glorious welcome she felt from her grandmother that New Year's Day.

The Nutcracker

The Nutcracker ballet is performed each Christmas by more than two hundred dance companies in the United States. It is the single largest annual moneymaker for most ballet troupes. Children grow up with this ballet being as much a part of Christmas as Santa or the tree. Television has made it possible for many more children to see and enjoy this magical Christmas ballet.

Peter Ilich Tchaikovsky wrote this ballet in 1891, based on the E.T.A. Hoffman story, *The Nutcracker and the Mouse-King.* It was first performed in St. Petersburg, Russia, in 1892, and though Tchaikovsky declared the ballet weak, the public loved it, and it was proclaimed an immediate success. It has remained so to this day, in Europe as well as in America.

Nutcrackers were popular toys when the ballet was written, and a story where wooden soldiers march, snowflakes and flowers dance, toy instruments play, and a nutcracker becomes a handsome prince who battles with a mouse, was irresistible to young and old. The ballet has a fairy tale quality, which Tchaikovsky incorporated with his theme of the search for love and happiness, and the triumph of good over evil.

The Nutcracker is the story of a little girl, Clara, and a dream she has on Christmas Eve. Clara received a nutcracker earlier in the evening, and in her dream, all the toys, including her nutcracker, are life-sized. A Christmas tree magically grows to an enormous size, and huge rats engage in a battle with toy soldiers. The Nutcracker Warrior and the Rat King are in a tremendous battle, and Clara, with help from mechanical dolls, kills the Rat King. The Nutcracker turns into a handsome prince and takes Clara to the Land of Dancing Snowflakes. Their journey then takes them to the Valley of Flowers, the Palace Terrace, and finally to the Palace Ballroom, where they meet the Sugar Plum Fairy.

Many versions of *The Nutcracker* have been done over the years, and new productions are done regularly. The music, dancing, costumes and stages are all magnificent, and the familiar music is a favorite during the holiday season. Anyone who is familiar with the music recognizes the tinkling bell-like sounds associated with the Sugar Plum Fairy dance number — the keyboard instrument used is called a *celeste,* and it was introduced in the first performance of *The Nutcracker* in Russia in 1892. The music and the ballet have brought pleasure throughout the world for over one hundred years.

The Feast Of Saint Lucia

In Sweden, the first day of the Christmas season is December 13, Saint Lucia's Day.

Lucia, who was born in Italy, was an early follower of Jesus but had been promised in marriage to a pagan. It was said her beauty attracted this pagan suitor, so Lucia, who did not want to marry him, had her eyes removed. She also gave her dowry to some of her fellow Christians who had been persecuted because of their faith. This so angered her fiancé that he reported her faith to the governor, who ordered her killed. While she was in the darkened prison awaiting death, she brought food to her fellow Christian prisoners, wearing a crown of candles on her head so her hands would be free to carry the food and water.

Many stories surrounded the death of Lucia. Some say she was killed with a sword; others claimed she was burned at the stake. One version reports she was to be burned at the stake, but the flames would not go near her body, so she was slain with a sword.

Following her death, Lucia quickly became a martyred saint in Italy, where they honored her by lighting huge bonfires and holding candlelight processions. The name "Lucia" means light and, since she became blind at the darkest time of the year, it seemed appropriate that they honor her with lights.

Saint Lucia's legend was carried to Sweden by missionaries. Tales of her generous deeds spread throughout the country; many claimed to have seen her miraculously ministering to the poor and starving. One account took place during a terrible famine in Sweden when people tell of seeing Lucia emerge out of the mist, on a huge ship laden with food. According to these sightings, she wore a white robe, and on her head was a crown of light. Older people claimed they spotted her in the early morning hours on December 13, gliding across icy lakes and snow-covered hills, laden with food and drink for the hungry.

The impact of Saint Lucia in Sweden was so strong the Swedish people commemorated her by establishing Saint Lucia's Day. First and foremost, it was a festival of lights, but great feasts were also held in her honor. According to the old calendar, December 13, was also the day of the Winter Solstice. Until this century, generous meals on Saint Lucia's Day were considered a good omen for a rich harvest the following year.

The tradition of the Lucia Bride began in Sweden, basically as a commercial endeavor in the 1920's. Shopping districts in Stockholm held outdoor Christmas processions led by Lucia in a white robe, topped by a crown of lighted candles. This "Feast of Lights" spread throughout Sweden, and soon every community and family participated in this celebration on December 13, each with their own Lucia Queen, or Lucia Bride.

In small villages, a Lucia Bride was chosen to visit each house with a tray of coffee and buns. Her brothers and sisters, also dressed in white, followed her, as she sang an old Italian melody, *Santa Lucia*, while walking through the village. Often, after people received their treats, they took a lighted candle and followed Lucia in a procession. Lights shone on all the Christmas trees in the village, and candles glowed in the windows — another symbol of the Christ Child as the Light of the World.

Traditionally, in Sweden, December 13 dawns as a dark and dreary morning. Early, as soon as the rooster crows, the oldest daughter in the family awakens, dresses in a white robe with a red sash and dons a wreath of greenery with nine lighted candles on her head. She stacks coffee and newly baked Lucia buns on a tray, which she serves in bed to each member of her family.

This custom was brought to America, where it grew in popularity, especially in Swedish-American communities. Contests are held each year, and on Lucia Day, a Lucia Bride is crowned, and the Christmas season officially begins with the "Festival of Lights."

Christmas Ships

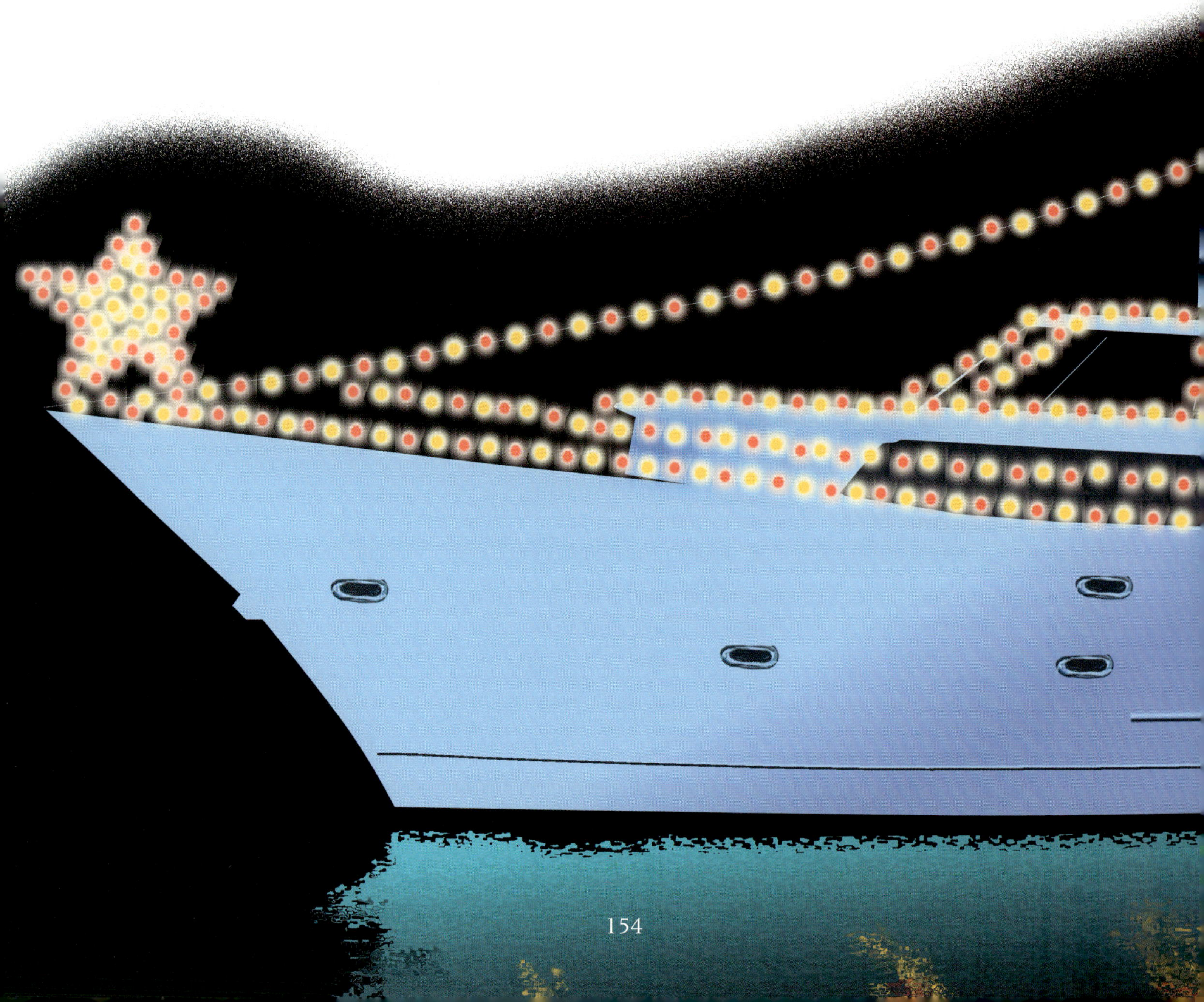

Winterfest
Fort Lauderdale, Florida

In the middle of the 1970s, a small group of friends in Fort Lauderdale, Florida, got together and decorated their boats for the holiday season. They invited other friends and family to join them on a cruise around the Intracoastal Waterways. This was the beginning of a tradition which today involves dozens of boats and attracts over 750,000 spectators. In addition, an annual television special featuring the boat parade delights millions of viewers.

Called *Winterfest*, this boat parade starts at Port Everglades and ends ten miles away at Lake Santa Barbara. It is held one night, starting at six-thirty, and the cruise lasts about an hour and a half. The lead boat shoots fireworks to announce the procession to follow, and the last boat is the Santa Claus boat. It carries the only Santa allowed in the parade … "after all, there's only one Santa."

Spectators line the banks of the parade route to watch every kind of boat cruise by. Boats must be at least twenty feet long to participate, but many are giant showboats or luxurious corporate yachts. They are often decorated with a theme, and guests are appropriately costumed to carry out that theme. Thousands of lights are strung, music is played, carolers sing and megaphones carry holiday greetings to those on shore.

Winterfest, a subsidiary of the Greater Fort Lauderdale Chamber of Commerce, has two staff members and hundreds of volunteers. The organization is primarily funded by corporate sponsorships and event revenues. In an area that rarely sees snow, this celebration helps the residents enjoy the Christmas season with some different trimmings.

After all, you can't do this in Nebraska.

Portland, Oregon

When December rolls around in Portland, people eagerly await the *Christmas Parade of Ships*. Meeting rooms, hotel rooms and restaurants along the banks of the Willamette and Columbia Rivers are booked weeks in advance. People who have their home on the rivers suddenly find a lot of friends who gladly come to a Christmas party during the time the brilliantly lighted boats cruise up and down the waterways. Bus companies offer excursions to view the event to senior citizens from all over the state.

People huddle for hours on the river banks regardless of the weather. They all come to see what Portland, Oregon, believes to be the longest-running Christmas boat event in the country.

The Christmas Parade of Ships began in 1955 when members of the Coast Guard Auxiliary decorated a single boat with sparkling lights before it sailed the Columbia River. Now more than sixty boats participate in the parade which takes place for about two weeks each December. Actually there are two parades — one sails the Columbia River, and the other cruises the Willamette River which runs through Portland.

Private pleasure vessels of all sizes participate in both events, and their owners compete to outdo each other in color, lights and design.

Members from eighteen yacht clubs enter their boats in the yearly event. Boats take a different route each night and their skippers must follow the leader boat. The board of directors from a non-profit organization plan the activities with great care. The *Christmas Parade of Ships* travels more than one hundred miles and logs a hefty 300 hours during the festivities each year.

Vancouver, British Columbia

The Christmas ships in Vancouver are called *Carol Ships*. The custom started in the late 1960s with decorated boats sailing three nights with carolers on board around English Bay and West Vancouver. A local tour boat company, Harbor Ferries (now Harbor Cruises), supplied one of their tour vessels which went out with a choir on board, broadcasting while the choir sang. The number of boats participating has grown, the celebration now lasts for seven evenings and the route includes False Creek. The Vancouver Tourism office promotes this attraction, and local radio stations support it. The parade is organized by volunteers who select different routes, and boaters may choose to join the parade for one or all of the night cruises.

A children's festival is part of the on-shore celebration watching the festivities. Spectators gather along the shoreline and build bonfires to heighten the enjoyment of the occasion.

Today, participating vessels are equally divided between commercial and private ones. The commercial vessels sell tickets so the public can come on board and see the sights during the nightly tours. Most of the vessels are equipped with generators which allow the owners to create a true Christmas ship with lights, decorations and music.

Poulsbo, Washington

On Bainbridge Island, Washington, a lighted Christmas boat parade takes place two nights through Liberty Bay, Manzanita and Port Townsend. Pre-arranged personalized messages are delivered from Santa to children along the route.

Seattle, Washington

Seattle's first Christmas ship parade was held in 1941 when a local boater led a parade of boats — without lights — during a World War II blackout. In 1949, the Seattle Department of Parks and Recreation took over the tradition, naming it the *Seattle Civic Christmas Ship*, which it remained until 1994. A private company, Argosy, then took over this seagoing celebration, renaming it the *Argosy Christmas Ship Festival*. Over the years, various ships have led the parade. The current leader is "The Spirit of Seattle," a 115-foot vessel donated by Argosy. This lead ship and two or three "follow vessels" travel to the departure point each evening and start the parade. Tickets can be purchased to board these lead vessels and enjoy the festivities. The festival, which runs from December 1 to December 23, has a dozen or so departure points between Tacoma and Everett.

A different guest choir performs each evening on the lead ship, and their songs resonate for miles to the hundreds of viewers lining the shores to enjoy the sights and sounds. Schedules are published in local newspapers so spectators in each area can gather to listen and join in the joyous Christmas songs while being warmed by bonfires along the shore.

Newport, California

In 1907, a group of visitors from Pasadena crossed Newport Harbor in a gondola decorated with Japanese lanterns. The skipper of this vessel was an Italian gondolier named John Scarpa, and the following year on July 4, 1908, Scarpa organized what is believed to be the first lighted boat parade. Scarpa's gondola led the parade, followed by eight canoes, all illuminated by Japanese lanterns.

In 1913 the parade was held again. Named the *Illuminated Water Parade,* prizes were given for the best lighted and best decorated boats. The annual event was interrupted by World War I, then rescued from obscurity by Joseph Beek in 1919. Except for several World War II years, it continued to be a summer attraction until 1949. That year, the city fathers of Newport decided the *Tournament of Lights* was drawing too many visitors, creating traffic congestion, and should be discontinued.

Fortunately, the Newport Beach city employees had decorated a holiday barge in 1946, installing a lighted Christmas tree. Passengers sang Christmas carols to the people along the shore of the bay as the barge was towed around the harbor. A ferry boat was later provided for the floating Christmas tree celebration, and gradually, other lighted boats joined the parade which became a popular annual holiday event.

Led by the Sheriff's Fire Boat, the parade sails six nights from 6:30 to 8:30 in the evening, and there are more than forty viewing sites along the route. Today, the *Tournament of Lights,* now the *Newport Harbor Christmas Boat Parade,* involves more than 200 boats, and has been hailed as one of the ten top holiday happenings in our nation.

In these cities fortunate enough to have a lake, bay or river, it is a truly magical experience to see these graceful vessels gliding through the water, bedecked from stem to stern with hundreds of colorful strings of glistening and blinking lights. They are like floating islands of light. The familiar and beautiful holiday music that floats to shore thrills spectators, young and old alike. Hundreds of hours are spent annually on planning and decorating the pleasure boats which take part in the parades. Spectators come from miles around to experience this unusual celebration of the season.

The weather can be quite inclement in December in the Pacific Northwest, but this does not deter the loyal and dedicated from making these parades part of their Christmas tradition.

Kwanzaa

December 26 — January 1

Kwanzaa is a celebration of African-American heritage. It has no religious significance, but is, rather, a celebration of life and values, a time for African-Americans to reflect on their cultural heritage. It emphasizes the strength and pride of the black community, and encourages each individual to redefine his or her own life and spirituality. Started in 1966 by Maulana Ron Karenga, a black studies professor in the San Francisco area, *Kwanzaa* comes from the phrase *Matunda Ya Kwanza*, which means 'first fruits' in Swahili, and commemorates the first harvest of crops.

The occasion calls for special decorations which are put up the first day, December 26, and consist of placing a straw basket *(mkeka)* filled with fruits and vegetables on a table. A candle-holder *(kinara)*, holding seven candles *(mishumaa)* is nearby. The colors used during the holiday are black, red and green; black for the beauty of the people, red for their suffering, and green for hope and the land. An ear of corn for each child is placed on the table, and each home has at least one ear of corn for the table.

The celebration is based on seven principles known as the *Nguzo Saba*. Every evening of the seven days, a candle is lit and one of the seven principles is acknowledged and honored. The Swahili name for the principles and the English meaning are: *Umoja* (unity), *Kujichauglia* (self-determination), *Ujima* (collective work and responsibility), *Ujamma* (cooperative economics), *Nia* (purpose), *Kuumba* (creativity), and *Imani* (faith). Each member of the family discusses the principle of that day, and what it personally means to them.

The first day is traditionally known as Children's Day and the last as Family Day. Many families drink only water or orange juice during *Kwanzaa* and break that fast on the last day when they all sit down to a large celebratory dinner. Family members discuss their commitment for the upcoming year, and simple gifts *(zawadi)* are exchanged.

Besides the celebrations in homes during *Kwanzaa,* community gatherings are held in local centers and churches. These occasions let people come together and enjoy songs, stories, fun, reflection and food. As in our Christmas holiday, food is an important part of the festivities. The Thanksgiving-like feast *(Karamu),* held on the last day, is a community-wide affair; ancestors are honored and many participants wear traditional African clothing and enjoy music and dancing.

Though this celebration takes place during the same season as Christmas, it is not meant to be an alternative to that holiday. A lot of African-Americans happily celebrate both occasions, but *Kwanzaa* has a special significance and meaning because it honors their ancestry.

Hanukkah

Hanukkah means dedication and is the Jewish holiday known as the Festival of Lights or Feast of Dedication. It is thought to be patterned after pagan winter solstice celebrations when bonfires were built to light up long winter nights. To the Jewish people, the fire or light became a symbol of holiness and rededication. Hanukkah occurs in midwinter, as did celebrations in many countries and there are similarities among most of them.

Hanukkah consists of eight days of games, singing, gift exchanging, delicious food and lighting of candles. It honors the victory of the Jewish people over their enemies more than 2,000 years ago. Hanukkah is usually held in December, but can fall in November, in accord with the Hebrew calendar, which is lunar and determined by the phases of the moon.

Hanukkah began in 165 B.C., as a celebration of the triumph of the Maccabees, a religious group of Jews, over Antiochus IV, a Greek king who had outlawed Jewish religious traditions, destroyed objects of worship and killed many Jews who defied him. When the Maccabees defeated Antiochus, they repaired and rededicated the Temple of God in Jerusalem, then held an eight-day ceremony, which was the first Hanukkah. The reason for the eight days may have been because they had missed their eight-day harvest festival *(Sukkot)* held in October.

Another story as to why it was an eight-day celebration is that when they relit the *menorah,* a seven-branched candle holder which is supposed to burn constantly in the temple, they had only enough oil for one day. But a miracle occurred and the oil lasted eight days.

Today's *menorah,* which is used for Hanukkah, is nine-branched, and is sometimes called a *hanukkiah (hanukkiyyah).* Eight of the holders are for lighting one candle on each of the eight nights of Hanukkah. The ninth is for the *shammash,* which means "servant" in Hebrew and is the "helper" candle used to light the other candles, and is usually set apart from the others by being higher or farther away. The candles are lit just after sundown on each night of Hanukkah, with family members taking turns lighting them. Forty-four candles are used for the entire celebration, and the candles must burn for at least thirty minutes. There is a specific order to the lighting of the Hanukkah *menorah* which is explicitly observed. Special blessings or prayers are said during the lighting ceremony. Two blessings are said each night; one is a blessing over the Hanukkah candles and the other one gives thanks for miracles. On the first night, a third prayer is added, giving thanks for being able to celebrate this holiday.

During Hanukkah, special observances are held in the synagogue. These consist of reading passages from the Torah on each of the eight days. Special events are held for the children including stories, concerts, parties and singing of songs.

Part of the celebration of Hanukkah is gathering the family together at least on one of the eight nights. Some families hold a special dinner on the fifth night which is called the Night of the Fifth Candle Dinner. The special gathering may be determined by the night the most family members are able to attend. Traditional foods are served, favorite songs are sung, familiar games are played, and most families exchange gifts.

Potato pancakes (*latkes*) are one of the most popular Hanukkah foods. The *latkes* are fried in oil, which is significant as a symbol of the oil that lasted for eight days in the rededication of the Temple. The recipe for *latkes* varies since many are family secrets handed down for generations. *Latkes* are eaten with sour cream and homemade applesauce. Popular treats are butter and sugar cookies, and cheese and jelly-filled donuts called *sufganiyot.*

The type of gift and frequency of giving varies. *Gelt* is a Yiddish term for money and is a common present given to children, though it may be in the form of chocolate shaped like coins. The coins are important, as they represent the first time the Jews were finally granted their independence and allowed to mint their own coins. Children frequently exchange hand-made gifts, and parents often give practical presents. Many exchange larger gifts on the last night of Hanukkah.

Dreidel, a game played during Hanukkah, uses a four-sided spinning top with a Hebrew character on each side. The characters, or letters, stand for four Hebrew words that mean "A great miracle happened there." That miracle was recapturing the Temple in Jerusalem after defeating the Syrians.

There are no historical or religious reasons to connect Hanukkah and Christmas, yet there are many similarities between the two, as there are connections to the ancient midwinter celebrations in so many different lands. The songs, the special foods, the gathering of loved ones, the exchanging of gifts are all part of the festivities enjoyed each year by those participating, regardless of the origin of that celebration.

To the Jewish people, Hanukkah is a time to remember and honor with their Festival of Lights, those who fought and struggled for survival and freedom. It is a special holiday that celebrates their being able to worship and live according to their laws and customs.

So remember while December
Brings the only Christmas day,
In the year let there be Christmas
In the things you do and say;
Wouldn't life be worth the living
Wouldn't dreams be coming true
If we kept the Christmas spirit
All the whole year through?

– Author Unknown

Epilogue

Christmas, as we celebrate it today, may seem far removed from the early ones we know about. But, as we have discovered, many of our Christmas traditions have been handed down for centuries, and are a mixture of pagan and Christian influences.

Most of the traditions have not changed throughout the ages, and are not likely to change in the next several hundred years. Traditions are our link with the past. They are the precious gifts from our ancestors that provide us ideals to live by and give us a sense of purpose. No other traditions are more treasured, more cherished than those we celebrate at Christmas.

Our fondest memories are most likely associated with our family. Decorating the house and the tree, baking cookies and other treats, buying and wrapping presents for loved ones, listening to familiar and favorite Christmas music, taking the little ones to visit Santa, going to midnight services on Christmas Eve; they're all part of what we remember from childhood. Celebrations in schools and churches, bringing gifts to the needy, singing Christmas carols — all lead to that wonderful Christmas feast, and the happiness we feel and express for this joyous celebration. Each year as we again experience the excitement of the Christmas season, the gladness, the love and the warmth, let us remember the reason we observe these cherished traditions year after year — it is the love of Jesus which is the very heart of Christmas.

Of all the traditions of Christmas, the best one is love.

INDEX
CHRISTMAS, TRADITIONS AND LEGENDS

A
Advent
    Calendars 41,141,142
    Wreaths 41,142
Ahwahnee Hotel 116
Alaska, Christmas Customs and Foods 37,117
Albert, Prince 85
Alfred the Great 6,114
Altadena, California 87,102
American Lung Association 147
Andersen, Hans Christian, *The Fir Tree* 95
Andersen, Hans Christian, *The Little Match Girl* 149
Angels 15-16,63
Animals at Christmas 25-31
Ara Coeli 21
Arthur, King 114
Augustus, Emperor 21

B
Baboushka 123,137
Baldur 75
Balthazar 10
Bambino 22
Basil, Saint of Greece 55
Bayberry Candles 72
Bees 41
Befana, Le 121,123,131,135-136
Bellingham, Washington 22,87
Bells 45-46
Berlin, Irving 65
Bethlehem, in Holy Land 10,19,22,41
Bethlehem, in Pennsylvania 37,85
Birds 25-31
Bissell, Emily 147
Black Peter (*Zwarte Piete*) 122,124
Boar's Head Ceremony 115
Boars, Wild 115
Boxing Day 55
Bracebridge Dinner 116-117
Brazil 72,123
Breads, Christmas 113
Brooks, Phillip 64-65

C
Calendar, Christmas 140-141
Caligula 55
Candlemas 41
Candles 6,41-42
Candles, Advent 41
Capitoni 117
Cards, Christmas 145-146
Carols and Carolling 42,46,63-65
Celts 73,97,114
Ceppo 101
Chimney 131
Chinese, Santa and Decorations 123
Christianity Outlawed 7
Christkindl 22,123
Christmas Tree Legend, The 89-90
Christmas Truce, World War I 65
Cleveland, Ohio 22
Coca-Cola Company 125
Cole, Sir Henry 145
Constantine, Emperor 5
Coolidge, Calvin 86

Corning Glass Company 102
Creche 21-22,85
Crib 21-22

D
Decorations 101-103
Denmark, Traditions and Foods 55
Desserts, Different Countries 113-118
Dreidel, a Hanukkah Custom 160
Druids 73,84,97,115-116

E
Eden, Garden of 85
Edison, Thomas 102
Eggnog 101,116
Egypt 5,13,16,72,84,111,114
Elizabeth I, Queen 55,116
Elves 123,125
Empress Hotel, Victoria, B.C., Canada 98
England 45,55,77,116-117
Epiphany (Twelfth Night) 10,41,55,84,142
Evergreens 71-80

F
Father Christmas 123-124
Feasts, Christmas 113-118
Festival of Lights 153
Finland, Traditions and Foods 117,127
Fir Tree, The, Hans Christian Andersen 91-94
Fir Tree, The Legend of the 95
Fort Lauderdale, Florida 155
France, Traditions and Foods 22,84,97-98,112,117,124
Francis, Saint of Assisi 19,21,63
Frankincense 10
Frigga 75

G
Gabriel 15
Garlands 55
Gaspar (Casper, Kasper) 9-10
Gelt, a Hanukkah custom 160
Germany, Traditions and Foods ..42,55,71,84-85,101,113
Gift of the Magi, O Henry 57-59
Gifts 54-55
Glassblowers 102
Glastonbury Thorn Legend 77
Grant, General (Nation's Christmas Tree) 87
Greccio, Italy 19,21,63
Greece, Traditions and Foods 6,41,55,72
Greenland 117
Gregorian Calendar 142
Grey, Sir Henry 114-115
Gruber, Franz X. 67

H
Hand Bells 46
Hanukkah 159-160
Hawaii, Christmas Customs 22,124
Henry III 55,114
Henry VI 6
Henry VIII 115
Henry, O, *The Gift of the Magi* 57-59
Herod, King 9-10,13,15,16,36,111
History of Christmas 5-8
Holboell, Einar 147

Holland (Netherlands) 55,123
Holly 55,71-72
Holy Family...21,72,111,113
Horsley, John C...145-146
Hoteiosho 21,124
Hungary 16,55

I

Icicles, The Legend of..105
Ireland, Traditions and Foods 45
Irving, Washington...116,124-125
Italy, Traditions and Foods 21,101,117,123,135-136
It's a Wonderful Life..15,46
Ivy 55,71

J

James I, King..116
Japan, Celebrations and Decorations....................121,124
Joseph of Arimethea 77
Juinisee 121
Jultomten 123

K

Kansas City, Missouri 103
Karenga, Maulana Ron..158
King's Canyon National Park..87
Krippe 21-22
Kris Kringle...121,131
Kronia 6
Kwanzaa 158

L

Laurel..71-21
Lauscha, Germany 102
Letters to Santa 125-127
Lichstock 101
Lights, Christmas 102
Little Match Girl, The, Hans Christian Andersen 149
Loki 75
Longfellow, Henry W...46
Lucia, Saint 142
Luke, Saint..3,22,77
Luminarias 42
Lutefisk 117
Luther, Martin...84-85

M

Magi, The (Wise Men, Three Kings) 9-10,19,21
Manger 19,21,22
Marks, Johnny..25
Mass, Christmas...6
Matthew, Saint..9,36
May, Robert...25,65
Melchoir..9-10
Menorah 160
Merry Christmas in Other Languages..........................143
Messiah 10
Metropolitan Museum of Art 22
Mexico, Customs and Foods...............................79,141-142
Middle Ages..6,55,72,101
Mistletoe..72-74
Mistletoe, The Legend of..75
Mithraism...5
Mohr, Joseph 67
Montgomery Ward...25
Moore, Clement C., *A Visit from Saint Nicholas*.............129
Music, Christmas 63-67
Myrrh 9-11

N

Naciemiento..21-22

Nast, Thomas..125
"Nation's Christmas Tree" 87
Nativity Scenes...19,21-22
New England...7,113
Newport, California 157
Nicholas, Saint.........................55,121-124,125-126,131
Nightingale, The Legend of..29
North Pole 125,127,129
Norway, Customs and Foods............................41,113,117
Nutcracker, The 151

O

Oberndorf 67
Ornaments 101-103

P

Padre Nicholas 123
Pagan Beliefs, Celebrations.........5,6,41,53,55,71,101,122
Palmer Lake, Colorado..37,98
Panettone 117
Paradise Plays..85
Pasadena, California 86
Peacock at Christmas Dinner..115
Peacock Lane, Portland, Oregon 103
Pelznickel, German Santa..121
Pere Noel..121
Philippines...37
Phoenix, Arizona...42
Pierce, Franklin..86
Plum Pudding..115-116
Poinsett, Dr. Joel..82
Poinsettia...72,79-80
Poland, Customs and Traditions...............................37,55
Portland, Oregon — Decorations 103
Poulsbo, Washington — Christmas Ships...................156
Prang, Louis 146
Prescipio 21,101
Puritans...6,7,46,77
Putz 21

R

Red Cross 147
Reveillon, Le..117-118
Richard II 6
Ring Dances...63
Robin, The Legend of the 27
Rockefeller Center..86
Roman Festivals and Celebrations 21,55,71-72
Romania, Traditions and Foods 37,54-55
Rome 21,22,41,71
Roosevelt, Theodore..86
Rosemary..55,72
Rudolph..25,127-128
Russia, Festivals and Celebrations........................113,151

S

Sanger, California 87
Santa Claus 120-138
Saturnalia 6,41,54,114
Scotland, Traditions and Food................................45,113
Seals, Christmas...147
Seattle, Washington (Christmas Ships).......................156
Ships...154-157
    Fort Lauderdale, Florida...155
    Newport, California 157
    Portland, Oregon 156
    Poulsbo, Washington...156
    Seattle, Washington...156
    Vancouver, B.C., Canada...156
"Silent Night"...67
Sinter Klaas 55,123

Christmas: Traditions and Legends

Sleighs 16
Spain, Traditions and Festivals 22,46,123
Spider, The Legend of the 13
Stars 35-37
Stockings 131
Strenae 54
Superstitions
    Bells 45
    Sun 5,71
    Evergreens 6
    Trees, Yule Log 98
    Candles 6,41,42
    Gods 6
    Spiders 13,107-108
Sweden, Traditions and Foods 55,113,142,153

T

Tchaikovsky, Peter Ilich 151
Thor 98,124
Tinsel, The Legend of 107-108
Three Kings (Magi, Wise Men) 9-11,36,41-42,54,84,135-136
Trees, Christmas 83
    Earliest 84
    Decorations 83,101
    German Influence 85
    Martin Luther 84
    "Nation's Christmas Tree" 87
    White House 86

Turkey 16,113-114,118
Twelve Days of Christmas 49-53

U, V

Vancouver, B.C., Canada (Christmas Ships) 156
Victoria, Queen 85
Viglia (Wiglia) 37
Visit from St. Nicholas, A, Clement C. Moore 129

W

Waits 64
Wassailling, Wassail Bowl 98,116
"White Christmas" 65
White House 86
William the Conqueror 55
Williamsburg, Virginia 42
Wilmington, Delaware 147
Winter Solstice 71,114
Woden 114
Wreaths, Christmas & Advent 55,71-72

X, Y, Z

"Yes, Virginia, There is a Santa Claus" 133
York, Cathedral of 73
Yosemite National Park 116
Yule Celebration 97-98
Yule Log 97-98
Yule Log Cake 98
Yule Dough, The Legend of the Christ Child 111